I0465667

BUILD

GROW

SCALE

REPEAT

THE DEFINITIVE GUIDE TO CREATING SUCCESS IN BUSINESS

DR. STEPHEN KALALUHI

Dr. Stephen Kalaluhi

BUILD GROW SCALE REPEAT:
THE DEFINITIVE GUIDE TO CREATING
SUCCESS IN BUSINESS

Copyright © 2019 by Dr. Stephen Kalaluhi

ISBN-13:
9781794003170

Printed in the United States of America.

10 9 8 7 6 5 4 3 2 1

DEDICATION

This book is dedicated to those who are brave enough to forge their own path, resilient enough to stand stoically in the face of adversity, and daring enough to follow their dream of living life on their own terms. This book is dedicated to those who look at the challenge of breaking with the status quo, and instead of cowering before it, say to themselves, "Is that all you got?" This book is dedicated to those who believe in themselves, those who believe they can build the life they desire, those who believe that success is on the other side of fear. This book is dedicated to those who have chosen to rise to the occasion, rise to the challenge, and rise to the great calling they have on their lives. This book is dedicated to those too stubborn to quit, too naïve to know the difference, too headstrong to accept anything less than success.

Dr. Stephen Kalaluhi

TABLE OF CONTENTS

ACKNOWLEDGEMENT

First and foremost, I want to thank God for giving me the strength to be the husband, father, and business owner that I currently am. Without His grace and favor, I would not be the man I am today. I must also give thanks to my beautiful bride of 25 years, also known as 1/3 of my Why. Without her support, prayers, patience, and occasional kick in the pants, my coaching practice would not have gotten off the ground. The other 2/3 of my Why (also known as my two sons) represent my heart and my soul. These two young men drive me to want to be better, not for myself, but to show them that there is better out there if they are willing to put in the time, effort, and energy to make it so. Last but not least, I want to thank you for your trust in me. There are tons of books on the subject of building a flourishing and thriving business. It is my hope that through these pages, you realize that you have within you everything you need to be as successful a business owner as you want to be.

Dr. Stephen Kalaluhi

INTRODUCTION

My journey to get to the place I am today was not an easy path. I faced setback after setback, failure after failure, and disappointment after disappointment. Although I realized at the time that the hardships I endured in the early stages of building, growing, and scaling my business were designed to strengthen my resolve and resiliency, it didn't make it suck any less.

But, as challenging and as scary as those early stages were, I wouldn't trade them for the world. Would I choose to go through them again?

Absolutely not.

But I also would not choose to change them. I now know those challenges and hardships prepared and equipped me to be the success I am today. I see it as my responsibility to pay it forward and share with as many business owners and entrepreneurs as I possibly can what I've learned it takes to build, grow, and scale a flourishing and thriving business.

Dr. Stephen Kalaluhi

Am I the foremost expert on building business? Of course not.

Are there more qualified people to write about how to unlock the secrets of growing your business? Absolutely.

Shoot, I can name four or five folks that I can point you to if you're ready to scale your business.

But here's the truth: Everything you read in this book is something I have either done or am doing in my own business right now. I'm not interested in sharing theory. I don't care about the latest craze pertaining to what you must do to market your products or services.

The insights and wisdom shared within the pages of this book represent tried and true practices that have made me as successful as I am today. Not only do I eat my own dog food and use the mindsets, skill sets, and behaviors contained in the pages that follow, I also coach and consult others to do the same.

That's why I love this book. Yes, you will walk away from this book with actionable and implementable things that you can immediately apply for business growth, but in the end of the day, all you're doing is getting a brief glimpse into what I'm doing in my own pursuit of building a world-class business.

You may not agree with everything in this book. I'm okay with that. In fact, I'd prefer you didn't just blindly agree with what I share. My preference is that you take what's shared in this book and test it within your own business. Take and implement a small piece at a time and see for yourself how powerful the strategies, Structure, and foundational truths are when applied to your own business.

I can tell you now, these things are going to revolutionize how you build, grow, and scale your business.

These things are going to blow your mind.

But here's a warning for you: Don't try to implement everything you're about to read in one sitting. Focus on Building first. Read through the five frameworks of business success and start by applying them to one team within your company. Use this team as a guinea pig to gain a better understanding of what does and does not apply. Then, when you've figured out what works in your business, simply turn on the spigot to full blast and have a great time.

A quick side note on how this book is sectioned…

The Build Section focuses on five foundational frameworks that must be implemented and mastered if you desire to build your business. Just like any Structure, the foundation is the most critical part of the integrity of the unit. If the foundation is weak, the whole building will collapse. But if the foundation is rock solid, you can build as high as you want.

The same applies to your business. Too many business owners are focused on growing and scaling but fail to establish a foundation strong enough to withstand the pressures and weight of that growth.

I personally believe this is the reason so many businesses fail within their first five years. They simply don't have a solid enough foundation to support continued growth.

The Grow Section focuses on the ten most critical drivers of business success and provides a blueprint for strengthening your business from the inside out. These drivers of business success uncover the importance of strengthening the mindsets, skill sets, and behaviors of business owners, their leaders, and their employees.

Without these key drivers implemented and continuously applied, no growth will occur, and you will see your profits, productivity, and efficiencies plateau at best, and take a nose-dive at worst. Creating an environment where the drivers of business growth are a part of your culture allows your business to flourish and thrive because its people are flourishing and thriving.

The Scale Section focuses on those activities you must master in order to successfully multiply your business. The key drivers of this section will help you identify those areas in your business you're most concerned with, because scaling and multiplying your business only exacerbates the short-comings you're currently experiencing now.

Then you repeat this process as often as you like until you achieve the results you're after.

Dr. Stephen Kalaluhi

My goal with this book is to give you practical and actionable items that you can immediately implement to reduce the stress, frustration, and overwhelm you might be experiencing right now. This book will give you a proper plan of attack to rectify what you're dealing with.

This is a book of solutions.

I am tired of talking to business owners who are struggling to make ends meet. I am fed up with watching business owner after business owner fall victim to the statistics. I get righteously indignant when I hear about another business owner shutting their doors.

And this book is me doing something about it.

You may not like me, and I'm okay with that. You may agree with everything I share. But like I tell all my clients, what matters most isn't that we're friends, it's that I get you results.

And that's what this book is about.

Results.

BUILD

Dr. Stephen Kalaluhi

MASTERING OTHERS IS STRENGTH.
MASTERING YOURSELF IS TRUE POWER.

- Lao Tzu

Dr. Stephen Kalaluhi

CHAPTER ONE:
THE FIVE FRAMEWORKS OF BUSINESS SUCCESS

"Let me embrace thee, sour adversity, for the wise say it is the wisest course."

- William Shakespeare

B uilding, growing, and scaling a world-class business that flourishes and thrives is hard work. Anyone who tells you otherwise is either stupid or is disconnected from reality. Either way, if you bump into someone who tells you that it's easy, run.

The truth of the matter is very simple: Building, growing, and scaling a business is one of the hardest things you will ever choose to do in your life.

Building a business has the potential to take every penny you have and convince you it's a good idea to pour it all into an idea or product. It possesses the uncanny ability to blind you to the reality in which you live as you pursue the possibility of what might one day become. This thing called business is, at its core, a gamble on your ability to manifest into reality what you see in your mind's eye, before you run out of time or money or both.

Now, those who figure it all out are rewarded greatly. The houses, the cars, the net worth, the lifestyle, the freedom. All the result of killing it in the marketplace.

But for every business owner who succeeds and is able to enjoy these fruits of labor, how many more fails? How many more lose everything? How many more end up with absolutely nothing to their name?

The Build Section of this book is dedicated to reversing the trend that so many business owners and entrepreneurs have accepted as normal. Too many business owners have accepted the Small Business Administration's claim that upwards of 95% of businesses fail within their first five years. Too many business owners are falling prey to this entrepreneurial epidemic.

In order to cure the epidemic that is business failure, we must first address the root cause of that failure.

Meaning, we must start at the foundation and work our way up.

Let's quickly take a 50,000-foot overview of the five frameworks of building a successful business…

FRAMEWORK ONE: STRATEGY

Strategy speaks to aligning the vision, mission, and goals of the company to each other to ensure each supports the achievement of the other.

Strategy is built upon a solid vision that explains why your business exists, an intentional mission that clearly states how you will achieve your vision, and specific goals purposefully designed to increase and improve your personal growth, your professional growth, and your financial growth.

Where most business owners' minds get blown is here:

Strategy, When Implemented Correctly, Isn't Just For the Owner, It's For Every Person in Your Company.

Every leader in your business, no matter how small or how big your company is, must not only eat, sleep, breathe, and bleed the vision and mission of your business, they must all have personal, professional, and financial growth goals that support the achievement of your company's mission, ultimately making your company's vision a reality.

I'll wait a second for you to pick your brains up off the floor…

You see, this stuff just doesn't happen in most businesses. If we're being honest, in most businesses, the only person who knows the vision and the mission, and who has goals to support the achievement of said vision and mission, is the owner.

And even that's a stretch.

Strategy, when implemented on purpose and with a purpose, has the potential to radically shift the trajectory of your business.

Imagine what your business would look like if every person who came to work tomorrow morning not only understood why they were there, but also knew how they were going to get there.

Imagine what your business would be like if every person who came into the office tomorrow morning had a specific goal to be better personally today than they were yesterday, to be better professionally today than they were yesterday, to be better financially today than they were yesterday.

Is that how your employees show up now?

Is that how you show up now?

FRAMEWORK TWO: STRUCTURE

In his book, *Good to Great*, Jim Collins provided us with a wonderful analogy of getting the right people on the bus, sitting in the right seats.

This analogy speaks to the Structure of your business and gives you a glimpse into what could be and what should be. In the sense of building a flourishing and thriving business, Structure speaks to ensuring everyone in your organization knows exactly what their role is, exactly what they are responsible for, exactly what is expected of them, and exactly how they are going to be measured for success.

Oh yeah, and all this is in writing. Signed. Clearly understood. And reviewed quarterly.

Most businesses fail because they operate on the premise that people know what to do, when to do it, how to do it, and by when it's due. Assumptions are dangerous and have directly killed or maimed more businesses than I can remember.

Strong foundations that build businesses are set against a backdrop of extreme clarity. What this means is the more clearly you communicate the roles, responsibilities, expectations, and measurements of each person in your company, the freer you become to build your business as you see fit.

Structure, then, releases you to focus on what matters most to your business. It creates the freedom you need to build, grow, and scale. And it provides your people with a blueprint to follow that all but guarantees their success within your company.

FRAMEWORK THREE: CHANGE MANAGEMENT

Of all the frameworks that successful businesses possess, the ability to manage change is perhaps the most crucial when the focus is on building a world-class practice.

As evidenced by their actions and approach to change, most businesses do as much as they possibly can to avoid it, and only succumb to change when they have no other choice but to change.

If you haven't already picked up on the theme I'm putting down here, this approach to building a business couldn't be more detrimental. You see, reactive businesses are constantly on their heels. They are constantly fighting to stay relevant. They are constantly wasting resources just trying to keep up. This is no way to build a business, and those who do find themselves in this situation quickly become statistics for the Small Business Administration to report on.

Successful businesses purposefully and intentionally put procedures into place that force change to happen. They review what's going on in the market. They look at trends in their industry. Most importantly, they ask themselves if what they've always done is still producing the results they expect to see.

Businesses that purposefully and intentionally create Change Management programs have strong foundations simply because they continuously challenge the most dangerous phrase in all of business:

"This is the way it's always been done."

FRAMEWORK FOUR: PEOPLE DEVELOPMENT

Perhaps my favorite of the five frameworks of business success, the People Development framework represents the single greatest and most critical asset you possess when building your business: Your people.

I firmly believe that if your business is plateauing, or productivity is slipping, or if profits are falling, it is because your people have plateaued, have slipped, or have fallen.

The success of your business is tied directly to the success of your people. The stronger and more resilient they are, the stronger and more resilient your business will be.

For reasons I still haven't fully comprehended, most business owners don't (or can't) see this correlation. When things start to fail, I've seen business owners yell, scream, pound their fists, and drop expletives I won't write about in this book.

Never once, and I do mean never, have I ever walked into a situation like that and had to answer the question, "How can I better equip, train, and develop my team so we accomplish our goals?"

Most business owners are quick to blame their people but are super slow to realize their people are a direct reflection and product of who they are as leaders.

Ouch...

Here's the thing: There exists an exponential relationship between successfully building a business and how much your people are developed, equipped, and prepared. Meaning, every amount of X you pour into your team, you can expect to receive back 10X in return. Invest $5,000 in the professional growth of each team member in your company and you will receive $50,000 in return. Invest an hour a week into mentoring one of your team members and you will receive ten hours more of productivity in return.

Most business owners don't see the return on what they invest. Most business owners don't even see it as an investment and only focus on it as an expense. But you can already see how this limited perspective can derail building even the most gung-ho of businesses.

FRAMEWORK FIVE: MARKETING

Building a world-class business is all about notoriety. The more famous your business is, the easier it becomes to build it.

Notoriety opens doors. It gets you in front of decision-makers. It creates proof that your product or service is worth taking my wallet out for.

Without notoriety, you will struggle to build your company.

Kevin Costner listened to a voice in his head in the hit movie *Field of Dreams*. He leveraged his farm and sold everything he had to build this baseball field smack dab in the middle of prime farm land.

The voice told him, "If you build it, they will come."

While this made for a wonderful story line and a great movie, following this advice is the beginning of the end for business owners.

You cannot serve anyone if no one knows who you are. You cannot sell your product to your target market if your target market doesn't know you exist. You must focus on increasing notoriety if your goal is to build a business that flourishes and thrives.

The key with marketing is to create momentum that draws your ideal customer to you.

Shotgun approaches just don't work anymore. They are costly, ineffective, and difficult to measure. When building a business, you must hold every penny accountable to creating more business.

If you're not worried about creating a return on your marketing, then you might as well throw your money into a fire pit…at least this way you can enjoy the warmth it creates as it all goes up in flames.

THIS IS YOUR RECIPE FOR SUCCESS

Baking a great chocolate chip cookie starts with finding a great recipe. But it doesn't stop there. Just because you find a great chocolate chip cookie recipe doesn't guarantee you'll bake a great chocolate chip cookie. You must discipline yourself to follow the recipe and not adlib because you think you know better.

The same can be said for building a great business. These frameworks for success are your recipe. Follow this recipe and you will strengthen the foundation needed to build your business. Follow the recipe in these pages and you will grow in every area that matters most. Follow the recipe in the next few chapters and implement everything you read.

And when it's all said and done, sit back, pour yourself a large glass of milk (or soy if you're lactose intolerant), and enjoy your chocolate chip cookies.

Dr. Stephen Kalaluhi

YOU MAY NOT REALIZE IT, BUT A KICK IN THE
TEETH MAY BE JUST THE THING YOU NEED.

- Walt Disney

Dr. Stephen Kalaluhi

CHAPTER TWO:
STRATEGY FRAMEWORK

"Always seek out the seed of triumph in every adversity."

- Og Mandino

T his book is all about challenging the status quo. It's about taking an idea or concept that most have fully and completely bought into and turning it on its head. My goal for this chapter is to bring you a unique perspective on what you believe is good business building Strategy.

The truth of the matter is most business building strategies fail to produce the results you expect and need. And it's not because they are bad strategies so to speak, but rather they are strategies that simply don't focus on what's most important to actually building your business. In this chapter, I am going to share with you the approach I take to business building Strategy for my clients and explain along the way why it produces businesses that are prepared and equipped to succeed in the building phase.

IT ALL STARTS WITH YOUR VISION

I know it sounds cliché to start a Strategy chapter using the vision of your business as a foundation. But the mere fact that this sounds as cliché as it does points to why it's broken and ineffective.

Let me explain.

Most Vision Statements are weak, ineffective, and impotent. They don't stir the hearts of anyone who reads them, and they don't cause anyone to rise up and say, "Hell yeah, let's do this!"

Weak Vision Statements create apathy within the hearts of the people of your company; ineffective Vision Statements create a sense of disdain for what your business stands for; impotent Vision Statements castrate employees and bind their hands from doing any real or meaningful work. What a Vision Statement should be is an exclamation that succinctly and clearly states why your business exists.

Take a moment and let that last statement sink in.

Why exactly does your business exist?

To make money? To increase your market share? To help you buy another house, car, yacht, or plane?

If any of these reasons above are currently in your statement as to why you're in business, I feel sorry for you. I feel sorry for your employees. I feel sorry for your customers and clients.

When your Vision Statement is self-serving and self-focused, you will ultimately fizzle out and fail. But...

When your Vision Statement is others-focused, when your business exists to serve others, when your employees show up to work every morning because they're in a culture of helping people, great things start to happen.

Let me give you an example of a Vision Statement that gets me out of bed every morning:

K2 Development Systems, Inc. Exists to Eradicate the Epidemic of Small Business Failure

Just reading this Vision Statement gets my juices flowing. It pumps me up and motivates me to get out there and dominate. But it's not just me. What's great about this vision is that it drives everything we do as a company. Every decision we make is run through the filter of whether it will help us achieve our vision. Every initiative we start is run through the filter of whether it will help us make our vision our reality. Every leader, every employee, every contractor we work with understands why we exist as a business.

HOW YOU WILL ACCOMPLISH YOUR VISION

This understanding is critically important because it is directly related to our mission. While the vision of your business speaks to why you exist, the mission of your business speaks to how you will achieve your vision.

Again, this is an area where most business owners fail. Because they fail to understand the importance of a mission statement, and don't see its relationship to their vision statement, they inadvertently and unknowingly build businesses that lack the integrity necessary to withstand the pressures of growth and success.

So, let's take a moment to address your mission. To clarify, your mission speaks to how you will accomplish your vision. K2 Development Systems, Inc. exists to eradicate the epidemic that is small business failure. This is our Why and speaks directly to why our business exists. Our mission states how we plan to accomplish our vision: K2 Development Systems, Inc. creates cutting-edge, world-class programs designed to educate, equip, and empower business owners and entrepreneurs to build, grow, and scale flourishing and thriving companies.

You can see the relationship between our vision and our mission, and how they are connected:

K2 Development Systems, Inc. exists to eradicate the epidemic that is small business failure by creating and facilitating cutting-edge, world-class programs that educate, equip, and empower business owners to build, grow, and scale flourishing and thriving companies.

I know I'm a little biased here, but this last statement is powerful. When I feel beat down, frustrated, or overwhelmed, I simply remind myself of why I do what I do, and who I am trying to help.

This is the foundation of building a great business. And I could stop here and make a positive impact on so many business owners.

But wait! There's more!

GROWTH GOALS

Now that you have a powerful vision and mission statement in place, it's time to granularize your Strategy so it involves every person in your business. Let's face it, your vision and mission statement are worthless if they don't move your people to act. In order to build your business, you must ensure each individual person is driven by goals that support both your mission and vision statements.

FINANCIAL GROWTH GOAL

Every member of your company must have in place a financially-based goal. For your sales and marketing team, this is a no-brainer. But for your support teams and those who perform tasks that are critical to allowing others to generate revenue for your business, their financial growth goal is more focused on reducing costs rather than generating revenue.

PROFESSIONAL GROWTH GOAL

In addition to each member of your company having a financially-based goal, they also must have a professional growth and development goal.

This goal applies to every person in your organization because every person must be better tomorrow than they are today. If your people aren't constantly growing, neither is your business.

You can't build a business if you aren't holding your people accountable for first building themselves.

PERSONAL GROWTH GOAL

Although your people spend more time in the office than they do at home, each member of your team must have a personal growth goal attached to their role in your company.

This goal can be whatever they want it to be: Going back to college, taking cooking classes, becoming certified in CPR, committing to working out more, etc. The personal growth goal is critical to building your business because your people need to know you care about who they are as a whole person.

Crafting personal goals that are discussed on a frequent basis brings the personal side of who they are into the workplace. When your people feel cared for, they are more willing to go above and beyond for your company.

USE THIS STRATEGY TO BUILD YOUR BUSINESS

There is a reason this specific Strategy builds business: It gets everyone involved, bought in, and taking ownership of accomplishing the mission and making the vision a reality.

Now let's talk implementation.

To start with, review your Vision Statement. Answer the question: "Why does your business exist?" Specifically, who does it help? Who suffers if your product or service isn't available? How does your business benefit your target market?

Once you've answered those questions, create your powerful statement: (Enter Name of Business) exists to (Enter Your Powerful Why).

How do you know your Vision Statement is powerful enough? It inspires you to want to do more than you're doing right now. It forces you to consider how much bigger, better, stronger, and faster you'll need to become in order to accomplish it. There is an element of "yeah right" to it.

If you don't need to grow in order to accomplish your vision, it simply isn't big enough. Go back to the drawing board and create a statement that makes people take a step back when they think of how much work it'll take to make that vision a reality.

I wake up every morning with the goal of eradicating the dismally high failure rate of small businesses in this country.

A big task, for sure.

But one I'm willing to fight for until I just physically can't any more.

Now that you have your vision statement crafted, it's time to move on to your mission. Remember that your mission is directly connected to your vision and speaks to how you plan to achieve your powerful vision.

I wake up every morning fired up and inspired to help business owners build, grow, and scale their businesses, and how I accomplish that is through creating, facilitating, and training those who are coachable and willing to learn.

Finally, combine your Vision Statement and your Mission Statement into one cohesive sentence, and this becomes your overarching business driving statement. This overarching statement is what forms the basis of the financial, professional, and personal growth goals of every person in your company.

This is where it gets really exciting, and this is what creates complete buy in from every level of your business. You see, when each person's financial, professional, and personal growth goals are tied to the overarching statement of your business, suddenly everyone becomes accountable, responsible, and liable for the success and growth of what's in their hands.

This creates an environment where everyone understands the role they play in achieving the vision of your business. This gives those in your company a greater sense of pride knowing they are directly responsible for building something bigger than themselves. This results in higher levels of employee engagement because they recognize what they are doing, why they are doing it, and for whom they are doing it.

Implementing this Strategy improves your capacity to build your business because it exponentially increases your ability to get things done.

GRIT YOUR TEETH AND SMILE. IN THE
FACE OF ADVERSITY, GO.

- Christine Lagarde

Dr. Stephen Kalaluhi

CHAPTER THREE:
STRUCTURE FRAMEWORK

"Adversity is like a strong wind. It tears away from us all but the things that cannot be torn,

so that we see ourselves as we really are."

- Arthur Golden

I love structure. Structure creates freedom. Structure unlocks potential. Structure is a wonderful key that gives you access to building your business as big, as wide, and as deep as you want to build it.

And this is what most business owners lack. Most business owners see Structure as something that slows the process down.

Something that hampers growth. Something that confines their creativity and ability to pivot.

So, they end up "winging it" in the hopes they are good enough to not need Structure. And before long, the stuff hits the fan, the wheels fall off, and they are so far down the rabbit hole that they can no longer see the light of day.

Implementing the Structure that follows will increase clarity, reduce frustration, and give you a peace of mind most business owners will never know.

And it's as simple as clarifying roles, responsibilities, expectations, and measurements (or RREMs as I like to refer to them as).

ROLES

When creating the Structure needed to build your business, the first question to answer is, "What roles do I need to fill in order to achieve my mission and make my vision my reality?"

Sales is a huge role that most likely will need to be filled. Having a Marketing team also makes sense. What about a Customer Service department? Or folks responsible for the logistics of distributing your product?

There are literally hundreds of roles that could be filled within your business, but the beauty of this Structure is that it identifies (and forces you to justify) only those roles that are key to actually building your business.

Would it be awesome to have a personal assistant? Of course! But is that role critical to you building your business? Maybe it is, maybe it isn't. I'm not here to convince you one way or the other, only to encourage you to consider the roles you currently have in place, as well as those you're looking to fill, to ensure they are business building critical.

Once you determine those roles critical to building your business, it's time to roll up your sleeves and get to work creating Structure. And it starts with putting meat to the roles you've already identified.

For each role identified, let's start by answering the following questions:

- How would you briefly describe this role?
- What qualifications are required to fulfill this role?
- How much education is required for this role?
- What special training or certifications are required?
- What experience is desired for an individual in this role?

Repeat this exercise with each Role you identify as business growth critical.

RESPONSIBILITIES

Most job descriptions are comprised of a Role section (to a certain degree) and the Responsibilities section (if you're lucky).

As you've probably already realized, there's a good way to build a business, and then there's a right way. When you're focused on the right way, certain aspects of what each role is responsible for comes to light.

Here is what you must do when communicating responsibilities for each of your critical roles:

- Provide a list of tasks each role is responsible for completing on a daily basis.
- Provide a list of tasks each role is responsible for completing on a weekly basis.
- Provide a list of tasks each role is responsible for completing on a monthly basis.
- Provide a list of tasks each role is responsible for completing on a quarterly basis.

If it's not clear yet, you can easily see how labor intensive the first two components of your business building Structure truly are.

This also speaks to why so few business owners ever do it. It's hard work. It's labor intensive. It's a pain in the butt. And, it's an absolute necessity for those seeking to build the Structure and foundation of a world-class business.

EXPECTATIONS

Let's shift our focus now to expectations, and how they play out in the framework of Structure.

As a business development consultant, I am often times called to help resolve conflict within companies. I do my best to stay objective and fair, and I do my best to listen with a filter that gives me the ability to stay impartial.

I've had the privilege of working with some of the finest business owners on the face of this planet, and after years of study and coding my own notes, the one common denominator that causes conflict, strife, and other unresolved issues is unmet expectations.

Let's see if this sounds familiar…

Someone on your team is getting on your nerves because they aren't doing what they are supposed to be doing. What makes it worse is the fact that they walk around like they have no clue as to what they aren't or are doing! They seem oblivious about their indiscretions and it only serves to make you even more mad.

This happens all the time in the businesses I work with, and the root cause is poorly (or never) communicated expectations. It's not enough to assume your team knows what you need. It's not fair to assume your people know when you need something done. It's not conducive to building a business to walk around your company expecting people to do what you expect of them if you've never effectively communicated what you actually expect of them.

That's why the third section of the RREMs is so important. It literally takes everything you expect of someone in a critical role and communicates it, in writing, so as to reduce and remove any questions, doubts, or misunderstandings.

This list of questions is more extensive than both the Roles and the Responsibilities sections combined, and with good reason. When you get the Expectations section clearly and effectively communicated, you take away any and all barriers to building your business.

Let's take a look at the questions you must answer in the Expectations section:

- How do you expect a person in this role to behave in meetings? On the phone? Communicating via email? When working with customers? When dealing with the public?
- How is a person in this role expected to dress?
- What are the expectations of this role in regards to physical appearance?
- What are the expectations of this role in regards to communicating with Core Team leaders?
- What is expected of this role in case goals cannot be met?
- What do you expect from this role in terms of professional growth and development?
- What are the expectations of this role in terms of building the team?
- What are the expectations of this role in regards to the success of your business?
- What are the expectations of this role in regards to achieving your overarching or corporate goals?

- What are your expectations of this role in regards to reporting and communicating progress?
- What are your expectations of this role in regards to reporting and communicating challenges / obstacles?

Definitely a deeper dive in this section than in the last two, but when dealing with building your business, I hope you would agree that ensuring everyone is on the same page and pulling in the same direction is tantamount to your success.

MEASUREMENTS

The last component of creating business building Structure is the measurement section. As you build out your expectations of the roles critical to building your business, ensure you take a step back and have a plan in place to measure the achievement of each expectation you list.

Here's the deal: If you can't measure it, it's not fair for you to expect it to get done.

Dr. Stephen Kalaluhi

Expectations without clearly defined methods of measurement creates too much room for arbitrary perspectives and skewed interpretations of success.

So let's look at a few methods to effectively measure whether your expectations are being met or not:

- Time-bound measurements
- Go / No-Go measurements
- Percentage-based measurements
- Task completion measurements
- Third-party review measurements

The key with creating measurements for each expectation is to get creative.

Let's say you expect your leadership team to attend professional growth training once per quarter. The measurement here would be strictly Go / No-Go, meaning they either did, or did not, attend training.

Or, what if you expect your team to submit their weekly reports to you by no later than 11AM each Friday. The measurement here would be percentage based, meaning how many Fridays did they submit their reports to you by 11AM versus how many they did not. Any tolerance you build into this measurement is completely up to you, but you can see how easy it becomes to hold your people to your expectations based on how you're measuring them.

Now, how do you measure the expectations associated with intangibles, like customer satisfaction? Simple! By sending a short questionnaire to the customer served asking them to rate their experience with your team member.

Anything you expect your team to accomplish or abide by can be measured. And it's vitally important to remember that if it can't be measured, then you can't expect it to be done.

PUTTING IT ALL TOGETHER

When these four components of Structure are implemented into your business building efforts, you are suddenly freed up to focus on more important things.

Think about this: What would it be like if you could tell a leader on your team that in order to be promoted to the next level they had to reach higher levels of measured expectations. For example, if you are expecting them to complete a task on-time 90% of the time, in order to be considered for promotion, they had to complete it on-time 98% during a specified time-period.

This takes the pressure off your shoulders and places the onus for promotion squarely on theirs. They either perform at the higher level, or don't get promoted.

The thinking here is if they're performing consistently at the higher level, then the promotion is deserved.

ADVERSITY CAUSES SOME MEN TO BREAK; OTHERS TO BREAK RECORDS.

- William Arthur Ward

Dr. Stephen Kalaluhi

CHAPTER FOUR:
CHANGE MANAGEMENT FRAMEWORK

"Every adversity, every failure, every heartache carries with it the seed of an equal or

greater benefit."

- Napoleon Hill

The most successful businesses are those who proactively address change, those who have systems in place to identify when it's time to change, and processes in place that drive leaders to review the Structure and Strategy currently in place to ensure it is producing what everyone expects it to produce.

The least successful businesses are those who are reactive, who change only when their industry forces them to change, and who fear change because it's too hard to effectively deal with.

This last statement is important.

Most businesses have zero process in place to effectively handle change, let alone one that proactively forces them to look at what needs to change in order to stay relevant and front of mind. Think about the "one-hit wonders" of the business world. The fads, the rising stars, the "here today, gone tomorrow" businesses that seem to pop up every now and again.

I'm sure they were all great ideas that had lots of merit. But I can almost guarantee you that what they lacked was the ability to see far enough into the future to make the changes necessary to stay out front.

So what happened?

They fizzled out.

Creating a Change Management program for your business will allow you to build your company as big, as wide, as deep, and as high as you want it to go.

What I love most about creating a powerful Change Management program is that is allows you to peek into the future. It gives you a fighting chance to adjust the direction of your business before it's too late. This is perhaps the most critical component of business building, and it is also the least focused on component of most business owners.

Most business owners are so focused on the now…making sales now, paying salaries now, covering expenses now, that they never stop to see how changes in their industry could impact their ability to do everything I just listed.

With a proper Change Management program implemented, you are guaranteed to be positioned to outpace your competition. Who doesn't want more of that?

You see, your Change Management program creates a formal process centered around how your business adapts to change, how your business reacts to change, and how your business proactively changes based upon anticipated industry events. Your Change Management framework provides you with the guidelines and direction necessary to be the change your business must have in place in order to flourish and thrive.

Let's take a quick look at a few key components of your Change Management program:

Process Opportunities

Every process, system, and procedure can be made better. A Change Management program will look at each process, system, and procedure and ask the question, "How can we make this better?"

Frequency of Process Review

The power associated with a Change Management program is found in how frequently you meet to review your critical systems and Structure. Too often these processes, systems, and procedures only get looked when the wheels have fallen off. By then it's too late. I suggest at a minimum setting these review meetings on a quarterly basis.

Process Strengths

Identifying the strengths associated with each process, system, and procedure allows you to justify why you do what you, how you do it. Communicating the strengths of each process ensures everyone is on the same page regarding why certain processes, systems, and procedures are followed and maintained.

How Does Each Process Achieve Your Corporate Goals?

Answering this question prevents you from relying on processes, systems, and procedures for the sake of them being there. This one question keeps you from falling into the trap of "it's always been done this way" and makes your entire Change Management program worth its weight in gold.

Process Threats

In addition to identifying the strengths of a process, a good Change Management program will also force you to look at the weaknesses of any given process. Answering the question of what could go wrong is almost as important as answering the question of what is going right.

How Can You Make the Process More Robust?

Once you've identified the potential weaknesses of each process, your Change Management program will ask you to shore up those weaknesses in an attempt to reduce risks to your business and to your growth.

THE CHANGE MANAGEMENT CHALLENGE IS REAL

Most business owners fail to implement proper Change Management programs for one reason and one reason alone: Ego.

Most of the business owners I've worked with in the past have built their business from the ground up. They've poured their blood, sweat, tears, and resources into making their business as profitable and successful as they possibly could.

While this is commendable on every level, what happens is they get attached to what they've built, and see it as a personal attack when anyone speaks against anything they've put into place.

I've sat in hundreds of board rooms where I've witnessed owners lash out at leaders who provide positive constructive criticism pertaining to making a process better.

Fool me once, shame on you. Fool me twice, shame on me.

What do you think happens when a leader within a business offers advice on how to make a process better, and ends up being publicly lambasted for their efforts? Of course, that leader is going to be hard pressed to offer advice again.

Which creates a culture where no one speaks up for fear of being attacked. Which leads to outdated processes, systems, and procedures that no longer work. Which results in a business that stops growing altogether.

In order for a Change Management program to be effective, you must effectively remove any and all personal ties to the process being reviewed. Once all personal ties are severed, everyone can focus on what matters most: How can we stay relevant and front of mind?

And that's how you build your business.

Dr. Stephen Kalaluhi

YOU'LL NEVER FIND A BETTER SPARRING
PARTNER THAN ADVERSITY.

- Golda Meir

Dr. Stephen Kalaluhi

CHAPTER FIVE:
PEOPLE DEVELOPMENT FRAMEWORK

"Prosperity is no just scale; adversity is the only balance to weigh friends."

- Plutarch

The most important asset in your business isn't the services you provide or the products you sell. And in spite of what you just read about your processes, systems, and Structure, they're not your most important asset, either. No, your most important asset is, and will always be, your people.

No matter what external threats come at your business, if your people are strong, developed, equipped, and empowered, your business will survive.

As critical as this component to building a great business is, too many owners overlook it, or simply forget its importance altogether.

Just like with the first four frameworks of building a successful business, developing your people must be intentional, purposeful, and consistent. Anything less and you open yourself up to shortcomings and failures.

ARE THEY REALLY MOST IMPORTANT?

When I step onsite to help a business owner build, grow, and scale their business, one of the first questions I ask is, "How much do you value the people in your company?"

I get all sorts of answers: "They mean everything to my company!" Or, "I wouldn't be here if it weren't for them." Or my favorite, "My people are the heartbeat of this business."

All great answers, for sure. But my next statement always throws them for a loop: "Oh yeah? Then prove it."

Most answer, "Um…how, exactly, do you want me to prove it? What do you want me to show you that would prove to you my people are the heartbeat of this company?"

While I make light of this situation now, it's important to recognize that what most business owners say isn't congruent with what they do. Often times this is most evident in how they develop, train, and equip their people.

Let's be clear: If your people truly are the most important asset you have in your business, it would only make sense to give them the best tools necessary to do the job; It would make sense to equip them with whatever training they needed to exceed your expectations; It would make sense to train your people to be the absolute best they could be, knowing that as the heartbeat of your business, the stronger they are, the stronger your business becomes.

Of course this all makes sense when you put it on paper, but the reality most of us live in, is there just isn't enough time in the day or money in the budget to support the training, equipping, and development necessary to build the people in your business.

Please don't take this as a judgment against you. I am here to share what I see across the large majority of businesses I work with. Where I will judge you is in the decision you make right now.

Now you know that your words are incongruent with your actions. Now you realize that how you've trained, equipped, and developed your people is inconsistent and unintentional. Now you understand why your people are so important to you building a flourishing and thriving business.

So let's get down to the brass tacks of what a powerful People Development framework looks like.

WHERE YOUR PEOPLE ARE NOW

A powerful People Development Framework starts by understanding where your people are starting from. The great thing here is that every leader within your business is starting from a different place. They each have differing perspectives, they each have differing upbringings, they each have differing belief systems. These differences make your business stronger, but they also represent a challenge for you in regards to the intentional, purposeful, and consistent training and equipping of your people.

Now, you can choose to create individual professional development plans for each of your team members and employees, or you can choose to broad stroke a professional development program across the board. Either one is suitable for growth as long as it is consistent, purposeful, and intentional.

No matter where your people are starting from as individuals, the goal is to create a singular goal they can all drive towards as a team.

WHERE YOU NEED THEM TO BE

It's important that your People Development framework address where you need your people to be. Purposeful, intentional, and consistent professional growth and development is only of value to you and building your business if that training equips your people to do what you need them to do.

This is where your Roles, Responsibilities, Expectations, and Measurements come into play. What skills do you need each person in your business to shore up, enhance, or sharpen in order to continue building your business? The answers to this question will drive your People Development and allow you to immediately see the return on any resources you invest in your people.

On a side note, this is one area where you should absolutely expect a return on every dollar you invest in your people. Knowing exactly where and how to invest is important to ensuring you receive your return.

WHAT IS YOUR BUDGET?

When your perspective on the professional growth and development of people changes from it being an expense to it being an investment, you suddenly recognize the importance of equipping your people.

Like I said previously, every dollar you invest in the growth of your people should immediately make a lasting and positive impact on your business.

So, what's your budget for the professional growth and development of your company's most important asset? Knowing this is an investment rather than an expense, how much are you willing to invest in your own business as you build out your company?

Talking about this number might be a bit uncomfortable, especially if you're still seeing it as an expense, rather than an investment. It's about to get a little more uncomfortable, however, because I'm challenging you to communicate this number within your business, and to create measurements that hold you accountable to making these funds available to those who you are ready to invest in.

IT'S NOT JUST THE MONEY

Let's be clear here: I'm not challenging you to just invest money into the professional growth and development of your people, I'm also challenging you to invest your time into them, as well.

You can set aside all the money in the world to equip and train your people to be truly great, but if they aren't allotted the time necessary to implement, to learn, to grow, and to build, then what's the point?

A wise person once told me that you can tell what a person truly values by two things: Their check book and their calendar.

If you truly value your people and you believe they are your company's greatest asset, your check book and your calendar should reflect it as so. Your check book should point to the monetary investments you make in your people, and your calendar should point to the time you've invested in their growth.

YOU SHOULD EXPECT A RETURN ON YOUR INVESTMENT

Yes, I've talked a lot about you investing your time and your money. But please be sure you hear me on this…any time you pour into your people and any money you spend on their growth is an investment. And with any investment, you should expect a return.

As you focus on building out your business, it is critical you communicate clearly and concisely what you expect from those you invest in.

The trainings you send your people to aren't days off from the office. They serve a specific purpose as it pertains to building your business. They aren't being rewarded with a few days at a luxury hotel while someone spews information at them. No, they are there on a mission to gather as much information as possible with the intention of bringing that information back to your company to implement it for greater increase.

By clearly and concisely communicating what your expectations are of those you invest in, you are almost guaranteed to receive back exponentially more than what you invested to start with. By sharing what you expect, those who are being poured into can ensure they are creating immediate returns on every dollar and every minute you invest.

Remember, when it comes to the People Development framework for building your business, if your people aren't equipped or properly trained, they won't be prepared to implement the growth strategies discussed in previous chapters. If your people aren't developed adequately, they will fall short of achieving your growth goals. To make matters worse, if your people are ready to build your business, your business will never grow any further than it is right now, and your odds of failing increase exponentially.

Build up your people, build up your business.

It doesn't happen any other way.

SOMETIMES ADVERSITY IS WHAT YOU FACE
IN ORDER TO BECOME SUCCESSFUL.

- Zig Ziglar

Dr. Stephen Kalaluhi

CHAPTER SIX:
MARKETING FRAMEWORK

"Show me someone who has done something worthwhile, and I will show you someone

who has overcome adversity."

- Lou Holtz

N otoriety. You either have it, or you don't. People either know about your services and products, or they don't. People either recognize your business as a major player in your industry, or they don't. Businesses who have notoriety possess a much easier path forward than businesses who lack notoriety. In fact, increasing your notoriety must become one of your primary growth goals as you continue to build your business.

Notoriety makes getting in front of your target market that much easier. It makes getting a meeting with a decision-maker that much easier. It makes building your business in general that much easier.

So how do you increase your notoriety and ensure everyone who should know about your business, does? Marketing.

Marketing is defined as the act of promoting and selling your products or services, including market research and advertising. If this sounds like a whole lot of words, you're not alone. What I take away from this definition is this: Marketing is how you let your target market know who you are and the challenges you solve.

Just like with the four previous frameworks, the marketing framework is built upon a purposeful and intentional plan that allows you to track the reach of every communication, every dollar invested, and the overall effectiveness of your marketing program.

REACH

Let's start by diving into a marketing term called Reach. Reach speaks to the number of customers or clients your marketing message has the potential to impact based on the market medium (television, radio, newspaper, social media, etc.) you're employing.

What's important to recognize here is that what works for one business doesn't necessarily mean it'll work for yours. You must find the medium that makes sense to you, test that medium to ensure it produces your expected results, then measure its effectiveness and reach.

FREQUENCY

Closely related to marketing reach is a term called Frequency. Frequency speaks to how often your marketing message reaches your particular target market. It's not hard to see how a marketing message shared once a month may not have the same impact as one delivered four times a month.

When in the building phase, you must consider the impact that reach and frequency have on the overall success of your marketing campaign.

As with anything worth doing, these things take time to do well, and your return on this investment may take months or even years to see. Measuring your marketing reach based on frequency gives you a clearer picture as to how effective your campaign truly is.

DON'T WASTE YOUR MONEY

I realize this last header may be a bit misleading. Building your business will require you to invest in a great marketing campaign. But here's what I meant by not wasting your money: If you aren't able to account for every dollar you invest in marketing, stop.

The mindset I have to fight against with some of the business owners I work with is this – everyone else is doing it and I don't want to get left behind. While I completely understand the premise and where this statement is rooted, I immediately push back and ask them how much money do they have budgeted for the trash can.

Of course, they all say, "None!" To which I respond by asking them to prove what they are doing in terms of marketing is actually producing the results they are expecting to see.

MEASURING MARKETING FOR SUCCESS

Every dollar you invest in marketing must be held accountable. Meaning, every dollar you spend must somehow, some way produce, at a minimum, two more dollars.

That's where measuring your invested dollar comes into play. How much does it cost to acquire a new client or customer? How much does it cost to retain the clients and customers you currently have? What does it cost you to gain referrals from the clients and customers you've already served?

These key measurements speak to the power and effectiveness of your marketing campaign. Meaning, every dollar is held accountable for producing more money.

Now, based on the reach, frequency, and media platform you've chosen, you can determine how much, exactly, it costs to acquire a new client or customer. You know exactly how many touches it takes to get them to pull out their credit card, and you know exactly how often they need to hear from you before they feel comfortable enough to pull the trigger.

Without concrete numbers in place, you have no way of knowing what's working versus what's not. Your guesses become costly and you simply throw good money after bad. This is one of the quickest ways to destroy anything you've built, and also one of the fastest ways to go broke as a business owner.

BUILD YOUR INFLUENCE

As you continue to build your business, focus your marketing efforts on increasing your influence within your target market. Increasing your influence, and thereby your notoriety, is as simple as adding as much value to your market niche on a consistent basis. As with any marketing campaign, increasing influence takes time to do well, but your ability to build something great improves dramatically when yours becomes a voice driving the industry forward.

For starters, post regularly on the social media platforms your target market uses most. Share your insights, share your tips and tricks, give massive amounts of value to those you serve, and be generous with giving your time and expertise.

These selfless acts will go a long way when building your influence, as well as your company in general. As an added bonus, the more value you add to the community you've chosen to serve, the more quickly you rise through the know, like, trust phases of buying.

The more they see you, the more value they receive from you, the easier it becomes to trust that you're not going to steer them wrong.

BE CONTROVERSIAL

Influence is often times not heard or recognized until you're willing to take a stand against the status quo. Take caution when swimming upstream, however, and choose to stand for something that you're passionate about and willing to fight for. Your passion comes through in the postings you share and allows for a deeper connection with those who find you through your marketing efforts.

TEACH, DON'T SELL

Your marketing strategy, no matter what sized budget, must include a teaching component designed to educate your target market.

The focus of your teaching component isn't on selling, and truth be told, shouldn't even contain a call-to-action or buy button. The purpose of the teaching component is to alleviate some pain point your target market is facing and provide them with training they can immediately implement to make their lives or business better.

Webinars are a great way to build rapport, establish relationships, and get in front of your target market. The best part about a live webinar is that it can be recorded and repurposed for additional uses.

UNDERSTAND YOUR MARKETING

The Marketing Framework is designed to open your eyes to what you're investing, where you're investing it, and how often you're investing it.

The days of blindly marketing in the hopes something sticks are long gone. It is time to hold every marketing dollar accountable for producing two or more dollars in return. It is time for you to measure the success and effectiveness of every marketing campaign. It is time to know exactly how much it costs to acquire a new client or customer, exactly how much it costs to retain a current client of customer, and exactly how much it costs to extract referrals from your current clients and customers.

Without this specific information, you're shooting blindly at a target you hope is there. Stop wasting your money and build into your business a sturdy marketing framework.

Dr. Stephen Kalaluhi

GROW

Dr. Stephen Kalaluhi

PROSPERITY IS A GREAT TEACHER; ADVERSITY A GREATER.

- William Hazlitt

Dr. Stephen Kalaluhi

CHAPTER SEVEN:
IT IS TIME TO GROW YOUR BUSINESS

"Adversity is a stimulus."

- James Broughton

G rowing your business is completely different than building your business. Building your business focuses on creating the frameworks necessary to stay competitive and relevant. Building your business addresses the systems and procedures that make up the foundation needed to flourish and thrive. Building your business sets into place the strategies that allow for continuous success and gives you the platform from which you can effectively grow, without having to waste effort, energy, or resources.

Effectively building your business with the frameworks, structure, and systems described in the previous chapters in this book frees you to shift your focus on now growing your business.

Growing your business focuses on addressing the internal characteristics of your people. It addresses the skill sets, mindsets, and behaviors of those responsible for implementing and adhering to what you established in your Build Phase.

Without this level of growth, your business will remain a shell of a company, and will never tap into its truest and fullest potential. Growth, based on improving skill sets, mindsets, and behaviors of your people, ensures what you built in the previous phase doesn't become an exercise in futility.

SKILL SETS

Every employee within your business possesses a certain level of skill needed to complete their daily tasks. Whether those skills are repetitive by nature or are tapped into only once in a great while, the skill sets your employees possess are critical to the success of your business.

It only makes sense, then, to believe that if you want to increase productivity, improve efficiencies, and generate more revenue, one would simply increase the skill set level of those responsible for the productivity, efficiencies, and profitability of your business.

This simple shift in thinking is powerful, and it's freeing. This new belief systems goes hand in hand with the People Development Framework in the sense that helping an employee become more skilled, is nothing more than an investment in the future growth of your business.

MINDSETS

Speaking of mindsets, the growth of your business is reliant upon the strength of not just your mindset, but the mindsets of every employee in your business.

You believe you will succeed. You absolutely must. So, your belief system and mindset are concretely set in the dream you chase hard after day-in and day-out.

But what about your employees? Are their belief systems and mindsets as solid as yours? Are they willing to do whatever must be done to succeed? I know you are, but how much growth will your business experience if you're the only one who believes in you? Chances are, not much.

Strengthening the belief systems and mindsets of those within your business is simpler than you think, but it's something that must be done purposefully and intentionally. Without a purposeful and intentional approach to strengthening the belief systems and mindsets of everyone in your company, you end up with an organization full of people motivated only by the clock.

BEHAVIORS

One of my closest colleagues loves to say, "Success leaves clues." And he's absolutely right. But not only does success leave clues, so does growing a phenomenal business. One area that provides the greatest number of clues is how your team behaves within your company. Behaviors are those things that create success, feed into strategy, and turn vision into reality. You can have a million-dollar dream, but unless you have million-dollar behaviors, they will never come to fruition.

GROWING YOUR BUSINESS REQUIRES ALL THREE

Without a doubt, growing your business requires you and your team to master every aspect associated with the skill sets, mindsets, and behaviors of success. Without these key components established, you will flail, and you will falter.

Getting these three components right allows you to grow your people as individuals, grow your departments as teams, and grow your business as a whole.

The next few chapters cover ten of the most critical drivers associated with growing your people, growing your teams, and growing your business.

Dr. Stephen Kalaluhi

ADVERSITY ISN'T AN OBSTACLE THAT WE
NEED TO GET AROUND IN ORDER TO RESUME
LIVING OUR LIFE. IT'S PART OF OUR LIFE.

- Aimee Mullins

Dr. Stephen Kalaluhi

CHAPTER EIGHT:
VISION-BASED DECISION MAKING

"Adversity tests us from time to time and it is inevitable that this testing continues during

life."

- Walter Annenberg

You need people in your company who aren't fearful of making the hard decisions. You need people in your business who understand what you're driving towards. You need people around you who are capable of seeing past their own emotions and personal biases to make great decisions.

The ability to make great decisions isn't something you're innately born with, it's a skill set that can be nurtured and developed for your benefit. Learning how to make great decisions is as simple as learning any other skill, but it requires proper training and guidance in order to make it powerful.

As you focus on growing your business, the importance of your clearly stated and powerfully articulated vision takes center-stage. All the work you did in the Build Phase of your business set you up to make powerful decisions that completely benefit your company.

Ensure that every employee within your business eats, sleeps, breathes, and bleeds your company's vision because your Vision Statement is the key to every individual within your company making powerful decisions that drive you closer and closer to success.

WHY DECISION MAKING IS BROKEN

The decision-making model isn't new. It's been around for years and will continue to be used by business owners who just don't know better. While I love the process and will fight anyone who says structure is overrated, it's critical to your success that you implement and follow a process and structure that actually works.

You see, the current model of decision-making doesn't work simply because it doesn't remove from the equation personal gain.

Most decisions made within your company are made on the basis of how it personally affects the person making the decision. How many people do you know who will make a decision that negatively affects them? I would wager that list is probably pretty small, if it exists at all.

We are inherently self-centered and self-serving. The current model of decision-making doesn't take this truth into consideration and gives the decision-maker free reign and all the space in the world to include their own personal prejudices and biases. You can only imagine how this process affects the growth of your business.

_ispossess

How do you combat and overcome the inherent prejudices we each possess to ensure decisions are made based on what's best for your business?

Simple. Make it all about achieving your vision.

MAKE YOUR VISION YOUR REALITY

Vision-based decision-making is powerful because it removes from the equation any personal desires or opportunities for gain. When your people are faced with a decision, no matter how big, challenging, or daunting, as long as they understand and comprehend the vision of your company you can rest assured they will make the best decision possible.

All that is required is they ask and answer this one question:

Will the decision I am about to make help to achieve our company's vision?

If the answer is yes, then there should be no qualms about allowing your people to move on their decision. But if the answer is no, then they either table the idea, or shore up the

Page | 96

deficiencies preventing the answer from being a yes. Either way, you come out on top.

When every decision-maker in your company bases their decision on whether it will help you achieve your overarching vision, your business cannot help but grow. This is why it's so important that every decision-maker in your company eats, sleeps, breathes, and bleeds your company vision. They must understand what you're driving towards. They must comprehend why it's so important to the overall health of your business.

So, get creative with helping your team memorize your vision statement. Give them incentives to not just memorize the statement, but to understand it fully. Challenge them when you see them in the hallway, and reward those who can recite it. Start meetings with what-if scenarios designed to make your people think about how they would respond and how their response might affect the achievement of the vision.

Like any muscle, vision-based decision-making must be exercised frequently and consistently in order for it to make any real difference. Use this decision-making process as frequently as possible to see the best results.

YOU DON'T WANT PEOPLE WHO NEVER HAD TO DEAL WITH ADVERSITY. YOU WANT PEOPLE WHO HAVE BEEN ABLE TO SUCCESSFULLY DEAL WITH ADVERSITY.

- Linda Ronstadt

Dr. Stephen Kalaluhi

CHAPTER NINE:
COMMUNICATING POWERFULLY

"Comfort and prosperity have never enriched the world as much as adversity has."

- Billy Graham

From a behavioral perspective, nothing is more powerfully connected to the growth of your business than how you communicate. The conversations you have, the emails you send, the text messages you fire off, if done well, stand as a solid foundation from which you can grow your business. But when done poorly, they possess the ability to completely thwart any and all attempts at becoming great.

The technology I just mentioned has made our ability to communicate faster, farther reaching, and more reliable. But it has also made us lazy, sloppy, and entitled as communicators.

The challenge is most communication isn't really communication at all. What we have come to consider communication is actually a one-sided attempt at sharing information. The challenge here is that no real communication occurs. Information is exchanged, but because communication isn't truly happening, there is no way to ensure comprehension or understanding is the result.

So, what happens is your entire company becomes filled with frustrated employees who have no clue as to why their team members aren't doing what they expect them to do. This frustration grows and it festers, and suddenly people are leaving in droves because they believe the grass will be greener working somewhere else.

Like vision-based decision-making, communicating powerfully is a muscle that must be exercised regularly and frequently. But it also requires an intimate knowledge of how to communicate in such a way that results in the growth of your business.

THE CURRENT STATE OF COMMUNICATION

Tell me if this sounds familiar:

It is Monday morning, and you just realized there's a mission-critical task you need accomplished by noon on Friday. You compose a wonderfully worded email with all the details necessary to complete this task and hit send. You pat yourself on the back for giving the recipient a whole week to accomplish this task, sit back in your chair and marvel at your awesomeness. Before long your focus shifts to other pressing issues and off you go to tackle the rest of your day. Friday rolls around and you realize it's 1PM. You check on the progress of that mission-critical task you assigned via email expecting to see everything as you detailed it in your email, but to your horror, you learn the task hasn't even been started! You fire off another email, this time heated, and you lambast them for not accomplishing the task you assigned them to accomplish. An hour later, you get this response: "I never saw your first email."

Unfortunately, this story unfolds in businesses more frequently than I care to recall. This exchange, and versions similar to this one, create confusion, cause unnecessary frustration, and

---

negatively affect trust levels within your company. And no one wins when the current state of communication isn't addressed.

POWERFUL COMMUNICATION IS A BEHAVIOR

As with any behavior, changing it for the better isn't always easy. Simple, yes. But implementing powerful communication within your business is bound to be met with snarls and doubtful employees. But as challenging as it might be to right the sinking ship that is lazy communication, once you get that ship back on track, there's no telling how far you can go.

Let's start with something simple that you can implement immediately as it relates to your electronic communication. Every email, text message, or other electronic form of communication I send to both my clients and team members ends with these two statements:

"Please reply to this message to confirm receipt. Also, please confirm you have no questions or concerns as to the contents of this message."

Think about what these two sentences do at the end of every electronic message I send out. One, I can rest in knowing the person I sent the message to received it and read the message in its entirety, and two, I can rest in the knowledge they understand what I am asking them to do.

What I love about this simple technique is it allows me to focus on what's next, rather than spending time, effort, and energy trying to determine whether someone read, understood, and comprehended what I needed them to do.

So, what happens if I don't get a response? This is groundbreaking stuff…I follow up. I take it upon myself to ensure the message I sent is read, is understood, and is comprehended. I make sure there are no questions, no concerns, and nothing that would otherwise prevent the task I need done from being accomplished.

This is what makes powerful communication powerful. It focuses on the behaviors associated with taking full and complete responsibility for the message being sent, the message being received, and the message being acted upon.

Most of your employees send out emails and fire off text messages, then wipe their hands of any responsibility associated with that communication.

They point fingers at those they sent the messages to when something goes wrong, and they are quick to blame everyone else for shortcomings and failures. Shifting the behavior to one of taking responsibility is what makes powerful communication powerful.

It takes time. It takes effort. And it takes you being comfortable with the uncomfortable. Businesses that are capable of making this transition tap into growth potential other companies only read about or dream about.

The question you must answer is are you willing to do what needs to be done, or are you willing to settle for what you currently have right now. The truth is simple: If you want growth in your business, you're going to need to stretch.

THERE IS NO EDUCATION LIKE ADVERSITY.

- Benjamin Disraeli

Dr. Stephen Kalaluhi

CHAPTER TEN:
HIGH- PERFORMANCE CULTURE

"You have setbacks in your life, and adversity. You can be discouraged about it or have courage to get through it and be better."

- Austin Seferian-Jenkins

Your mindsets and belief systems drive everything your business has accomplished to date, is accomplishing in the here and now, and will ever accomplish moving forward. In fact, your growth as a business is limited only by what you and your team believe you can achieve. From a mindset perspective, nothing empowers your people to grow more than creating a high-performance culture.

Because so few people have actually experienced a high-performance culture, few people understand what it actually takes to create one.

There are five mindsets you and your people must master in order to grow your business. These mindsets include problem solving, knowing how to rally your people around a common goal, trusting that collaboration is far more effective than going at it alone, simplifying strategy, and the importance of momentum.

THE PROBLEM-SOLVING MINDSET

There are two types of people in this world: Those who only see problems, and those who only see opportunities. Obviously, you want to surround yourself with those who see the opportunities, rather than those who see the problems, but the challenge is finding those people.

What if, instead of having to find them and hire them, you could help those already in your business to become them?
High-performance culture is naturally created when every person within your organization focuses on what could be and

what should be, rather than on what is. And this focus is the direct result of the culture you create.

Let's remember that company culture is created based on what you celebrate, as well as what you ignore. If you ignore people who show up late for work, you'll inadvertently create a culture of employees who believe it's okay to cut corners. But if you reward those who consistently arrive before their scheduled start time, you'll eventually create a culture where promptness is the norm.

The same holds true for problem-solving. If you give attention and time to those who constantly complain about what's not working and how awful things are, you will inadvertently create a culture where everyone complains. However, if you reward those who, instead of complaining, actually create solutions, you will build a culture where employees are encouraged to solve problems, rather than just be one.

This simple shift in thinking is all it takes to create a high-performance culture. Your mindset when it comes to problems dictates how those around you react.

What if you're the problem? Well…make the change and make it now. Ask someone you trust to hold you accountable for focusing on those things you want to reward. Your mindset and your belief system will drive everyone else's in your company.

THE RALLYING MINDSET

What's the easiest way to shift the culture in your business for the better? Make sure everyone is onboard, understands the Why behind the transformation, and can see exhibited in you the behaviors you want to see exhibited in them.

A mindset that is concerned with rallying your team creates a culture where employees are engaged, where they feel like they are shifting the culture together rather than it happening to them, and where they are connected to a cause greater than just themselves.

High-performance culture is the result of high-performance employees. High-performance employees are the result of company cultures that support and encourage their engagement.

THE COLLABORATION MINDSET

Long gone are the lone-ranger days of going at it alone. The "I work better by myself" mantra is merely a blip on our historical radar. Growing your company requires your people to work well together, to achieve more as a unit, and to collaborate effectively across every department and role.

Although it's obvious you can go further together than you can alone, shifting the culture of your company to reflect this belief means celebrating teamwork and collaborative efforts.

Think and speak in terms of "us" and "we," rather than "you" or "I." This simple shift in thinking creates an environment where it's uncomfortable to work alone, where being a part of a team is celebrated, and where collaborative efforts are the norm.

The more your teams are able to accomplish together, the more they will seek each other out to accomplish more. Allow the collaboration culture and its success to fuel the growth of your business.

THE SIMPLIFIED STRATEGY MINDSET

Strategy used to be reserved for the Executive Level leaders of an organization. So much so that this belief system still unknowingly permeates businesses today. The root of this culture-killer is founded upon the idea that knowledge is power, and the more knowledge I have, the more power I have.

In order to maintain the different levels of influence, executives would keep strategy to themselves, and only share on a need-to-know basis. Naturally, this creates a rift and divide within an organization, and the culture that springs up as a result of this divide supports it.

Growing your business will not happen if there are divisions within your organization. Creating a high-performance culture requires you to openly and freely share your strategy for business growth.

This might seem off to you, but answer this question:

How can your people achieve the company's vision if they aren't privy to the strategy you're using to achieve it?

The answer, of course, is they can't.

And the only reason most business owners don't share their business growth strategy is because they don't see how detrimental it is to keep it from those responsible for making it happen.

Shifting your mindset to a belief system that supports as many people within your company knowing about your strategy is the first step to creating a high-performance culture. This shift will naturally result in a greater level of overall growth.

THE MOMENTUM MINDSET

Most businesses fail, not because they lack the skill sets, mindsets, and behaviors necessary to succeed, but because they fall into a rut and lose momentum.

Often times this failure is the direct result of losing sight of your Why. When you lose sight of why you do what you do, work becomes mundane and without purpose. Your employees start going through the motions and do just enough to not get fired.

Your productivity wavers and you fall into the trap of believing this is as good as it's going to get.

Creating a high-performance culture means consistently and constantly reminding your people why they are doing what they are doing. It's about ensuring they know whom their work affects. It's about putting names and faces to the customers and clients you serve.

This shift in mindset and belief systems give you the fuel necessary to drive your culture forward. It gives your people something to believe in. And it allows your business to stay connected to something bigger than any one person.

I AM A BIG BELIEVER IN OVERCOMING AND ACHIEVING AND DOING THINGS AND NOT FEELING SORRY FOR YOURSELF.

- Drew Carey

Dr. Stephen Kalaluhi

CHAPTER ELEVEN:
ENHANCING TRUST

"The greater the obstacle, the more glory in overcoming it."

- Moliere

Enhancing trust within your business is one of the most important endeavors you will ever be responsible for as an owner. In his book *The Speed of Trust*, Stephen Covey takes a deep dive into the construct of trust and how it factors into your success as a business owner.

There are literally tomes of research, anecdotal evidence, and popular press material printed on the importance of trust to organizational success, but yet trust is just as pervasive in businesses today as it was more than a decade ago when *The Speed of Trust* was first published.

I firmly believe that the challenge facing business owners isn't the knowledge associated with the importance of building trust, but rather it's the "how" associated with the actions that actually result in increased trust.

Trust is one of those remarkable constructs that can be found in all three components of growing your business. An argument can be made that building trust is a skill set that can and should be learned and mastered. Others could argue that enhanced trust is the result of the right behaviors exhibited at the right times. Still others could make the argument that strengthening trust starts with strengthening the mindsets and belief systems that govern trust within businesses.

To all those who might make such an argument, I say you are absolutely right. Trust knows no boundaries and must be addressed from the perspective of learning a new skill set, from the perspective of mastering trust enhancing behaviors, and from the perspective of changing mindsets and belief systems to allow for trust to grow.

What this really means is enhancing trust isn't as cut and dry as some would lead you to believe. The complexity of this construct and how it intertwines itself throughout the very fabric of your business gives me pause when I think about sharing advice because every business is different, and every situation requires a different approach.

With that caveat out of the way, however, here are seven things you can do right now to enhance the levels of trust within your company:

#1: TRULY KNOW YOUR PEOPLE

The biggest challenge you face when growing your business is establishing strong enough relationships with those you are working side by side with. Most business owners shy away from broaching the personal side of the people on their team, simply because they don't know how to broach it.

Great business owners, however, successfully merge the two by setting ground rules and boundaries that let their people know when it's appropriate to discuss their personal lives and when it's time to focus on getting stuff done.

The more you know your people, and the more they know you, the easier it becomes to strengthen the trust you already have and develop even more.

#2: ASSESS YOUR RELATIONSHIPS

The challenge you face in growing your business is your perceptions versus your realities. The area this affects your business the most is in the strength of the relationships you have with those you work with daily.

You believe you have a strong relationship, but in reality, your team can barely stand you. Being real with yourself and the strength of the relationships you have with your people is a critical component of growing your business.

Here's the thing: If you aren't open to assessing your current relationships, then you won't be open to doing what it's going to take to improve those relationships. Great business owners take the time necessary to reflect on the strength of each relationship so they can better understand what needs to be improved upon and how it affects the levels of trust within the company.

#3: STRENGTHEN YOUR RELATIONSHIPS

Enhancing trust within your business to the point it can grow your company is the result of actions you take daily. One action that delivers a massive return on your investment is purposefully and intentionally strengthening the relationships you have with your people.

Grab a cup of coffee, or maybe even a beer. Share your story around why you started your company. Ask them to share with you why they like working for you. Get creative, ask a lot of questions, and be a great listener.

The key with strengthening relationships is the fact it cannot be rushed, and it cannot be fake. Rushing a relationship will only serve to set it back further, and inauthentic attempts at building trust can be spotted a mile away.

#4: FOCUS ON THE INDIVIDUAL

Here's one trust-building exercise that throws most business owners for a loop: Remember that your team is comprised of individuals who require you to build relationships with them individually.

While small group settings are more comfortable, there's nothing that can take the place of a one-on-one conversation when it comes to enhancing trust.

Also, there is no faster way to establish trust than by spending quality one-on-one time someone. So, if growing your business is the goal, and you realize this won't happen without your people trusting you, simply schedule as many one-on-one sessions as you can, as frequently as you can, until your team knows enough about you to fully trust you have their best interests at heart.

#5: GET FEEDBACK REGULARLY

Notice I didn't say *give* feedback. I said *get* feedback. One of the things that all but disappears when you go into business for yourself is a trusted voice who isn't scared of telling you how crazy or stupid you're being.

And let's face it, most of your employees simply don't trust you enough to give you honest feedback even when you need it most.

To combat this unfortunate truth, I want to encourage you to make regular space to receive and address feedback from those within your business you trust most. Schedule recurring time on your calendar so you can have one-on-one sessions with two or three people you trust, and ask them to answer this one question:

What can I do to be better tomorrow than I am today?

Structuring the question in this way keeps the energy positive. And giving this structure to those providing you with feedback allows them to share opportunities for growth with you, in a way that isn't degrading or condescending. This approach strengthens relationships and enhances trust, allowing you to focus on growing your business.

VERY RARELY DO YOU HAVE A PERFECT RACE.
IT IS ABOUT OVERCOMING YOUR MISTAKES IN
THE RACE AND REMAINING COMPOSED.

- Allen Johnson

Dr. Stephen Kalaluhi

CHAPTER TWELVE:
DELEGATING WITH AUTHORITY

"All the world is full of suffering. It is also full of overcoming."

- Helen Keller

P erhaps the greatest foe of any growing business is the inability to delegate. I get it. You poured your blood, sweat, tears, and money into building something of value. You spent countless hours and more sleepless nights than you can remember do everything and anything to secure the success of your business. And now that you have a solid foundation set and your business is growing, the scariest thing you're faced with is the prospect of letting go and giving someone else control of the reins.

As it pertains to growing your business, however, you're in luck because delegation is a skill set. And it being a skill set means you can learn to do it well if you're willing to invest the time to do it well.

Let's focus on what delegating with authority looks like as you continue to grow your business...

LET IT GO

The first step in mastering delegation is to get comfortable with being uncomfortable. Yes, it's truly uncomfortable the first time you give control to someone other than yourself. Shoot, it's uncomfortable no matter how many times you delegate. But the more trust you establish within those you lead, the more confident you will become in their ability to not only get the job done, but to fully appreciate your vision and your motivations.

When first learning to get comfortable with delegating, start small. Give your team small tasks that aren't mission-critical and gauge how they handled the assignment.

Did they knock it out of the park? Did they miss a few things that caught your eye? Did they completely miss the mark?

Regardless of how well or how miserably your team performs a task, it's important to remember that it's a reflection on you, not them. Meaning, if they did well, it's because of you. However, if they missed something, or they failed horribly, it's because you didn't train them well.

Being comfortable delegating starts with a solid program for transferring knowledge from your head and heart into their hands.

PRIORITIZE DELEGATED TASKS

The more comfortable you become delegating tasks, the more tasks you will delegate. As you learn to trust your team with specific tasks, it's important to remember to prioritize for them which tasks are more important than others.

This falls into the realm of training, but it also speaks to your ability to communicate powerfully. When giving your team more than one task to accomplish, it's crucial that you do as much thinking for them as possible.

Don't leave anything up to them to decipher. They will never succeed if you're leaving them to read between the lines. Be clear in what needs to be completed first, what needs attention second, and what can wait until the following day, if necessary.

Not only does the process of prioritizing delegated tasks give you peace of mind as a business owner growing your business, it gives your team members confidence knowing they are doing exactly what you expect to get done.

KNOW YOUR TEAM

Getting to know your team better is the natural byproduct of enhancing trust. But it also allows you to recognize their individual strengths, giftings, talents, and abilities.

For example, if you spent any amount of time getting to know me better, you'd realize quickly that I do not enjoy administrative work.

Filing, organizing, alphabetizing, formatting...these are all things I do because I have to, but they are also things I would give up in a heartbeat if someone even looked like they wanted to take it from me.

Armed with this knowledge, it would be asinine for you to delegate an administrative-based project to me. Would I do it? Of course! Would I hate every minute of it? Absolutely.

Knowing who your people are allows you to delegate tasks to those who not only possess the skill sets, mindsets, and behaviors to do it well, but who will enjoy the task overall.

GIVE CLEAR DIRECTIONS

Giving your team anything less than crystal clear directions is a failure on your part. Growing your business cannot be left to misunderstandings or misinterpretations. Your responsibility when delegating to your team is communicating in such a way that removes any and all ambiguity from the equation. There should be zero questions, no room for doubt, and clarity around what you expect.

TRAIN YOUR TEAM

This should go without saying, but you cannot expect your team to succeed if they aren't properly trained and equipped to succeed. In fact, delegating a task to your team without first giving them the proper tools and training to accomplish the task will only serve to frustrate them and burn you.

This is scary to some business owners, but the truth is everything you know how to do, your team should also know how to do. Whether it's sales, customer-service, manufacturing, logistics, technical knowledge…everything you know, they should know.

Duplicating yourself by sharing and transferring your knowledge is the truest form of growing your business.

TRUST, BUT VERIFY

Inspect everything your team does. Not for the purpose of finding errors, but for the purpose of identifying opportunities for growth. You are responsible for everything that comes from your team. Creating milestones and checkpoints for the work you delegate allows you to monitor progress and ensure everyone is staying focused.

Scheduled check-ins are powerful tools that give you the ability to delegate while simultaneously keeping a tight leash on the project as a whole. Check-ins force team members to provide progress updates, as well as gives them an opportunity to share concerns, ask for guidance, or request additional support.

Trusting your team to accomplish a delegated task is one thing, but verifying the quality of said work is something completely different. The goal is to eventually raise up leaders within your company who know you and what you expect so well that they are able to be your source of verification.

Dr. Stephen Kalaluhi

IT IS PART OF LIFE TO HAVE OBSTACLES. IT IS ABOUT OVERCOMING OBSTACLES...THAT IS THE KEY TO HAPPINESS.

- Herbie Hancock

Dr. Stephen Kalaluhi

CHAPTER THIRTEEN:
CREATING POSITIVE CONFLICT

"There's nothing like overcoming something that scares you so much. Nothing feels better."

- Laura Wilkinson

Conflict within businesses has gone off the rails. A recent report stated 3 out of 4 employees surveyed would rather change their boss than take a pay raise. The research found that 8 out of 10 employees had little to no trust in their leaders. And if it couldn't get worse, 1 out of every 4 employees surveyed stated they burned a sick day just to avoid the negative effects of conflict at work.

Conflict at work costs U.S. based businesses more than $300 billion in lost time and productivity, turnover due to an inability to resolve issues, and litigation of employee claims.

To say conflict within your company is a threat to the growth of your business would be an understatement. But every day, employees across the nation silently suffer as they walk into companies that are unable to resolve conflict.

As it was with trust, creating positive conflict spans all three of the components of skill sets, mindsets, and behaviors. This one construct is so important that if this was the only thing you did to grow your business, you'd be heads and shoulders above your competition.

The secret here isn't to remove conflict from within your business, but rather to funnel it into something that produces growth and increase. It's understanding from where conflict stems and learning how to turn it into something positive.

Once you learn how to turn the negative effects of conflict into positive organizational growth, you and your people will actually welcome conflict because you'll recognize it as the precursor to the growth of your business.

KEEP DIALOGUE GOING

One of the main reasons conflict results in so much negativity and lost revenue for businesses is because communication ceases when a person is in the midst of conflict.

A quick side note: Being in the midst of conflict doesn't mean two or more people are at odds. An individual with perceived hurts or slights could be in the midst of conflict without anyone else being involved or even aware.

But I digress...

When communication breaks down, there is no chance for the conflict to be resolved. But as human beings, we have very little training when it comes to effectively and positively dealing with conflict. So instead of facing it head on and trying to figure everything out, we typically choose to ignore the situation and ignore the person who offended us.

When we consciously choose to ignore the situation and the person who offended us, we automatically shut down any and all communication.

When communication stops, so does any chance of resolving conflict. And it festers. And starts to boil up inside you. Until one day you just can't control it and you lose it.

Turning conflict in your business into something that results in growth is as simple as making a conscious decision that no matter how hard things might seem, you're going to keep the lines of communication open.

ACTIVELY LISTEN

Now that you've made the conscious decision to keep the lines of communication open, the next step for those in conflict is to commit to active listening.

Active listening requires those in conflict to remain present, to not day-dream, to stay focused on what the other person (or people) is saying. It's important to recognize that active listening is not a skill set that comes naturally to most people.

It requires people to ask clarifying questions, ask probing questions, and to not let go of those issues until they are fully and completely resolved.

Remember, active listening doesn't mean you have to agree with everything the other person is saying. It means you're willing and open to understand what the other person is saying, feeling, and perceiving.

FOCUS ON THE PROCESS

This key is perhaps the most critical to turning the negative effects of conflict into business growth. You see, conflict usually stems from a disagreement on process, then quickly escalates because the disagreement is taken as a personal attack.

When the focus of a conflict within your business shifts from being about a person to being about what is best for your company, those involved are more apt to hear what others have to say. When it is not about any one person, all the history and all the drama associated with typical conflict is removed. This allows both sides of the conflict to focus on what is best for the company, rather than on what is best for them.

AGREE TO DISAGREE

Resolving conflict and turning it into positive growth for your business does not necessarily mean everyone agrees. On the contrary, positive conflict allows for disagreements to occur. The ability to disagree but still move forward is the surest sign of positive conflict within your business.

The ability to disagree also speaks to the health of the leaders within your business. One recipe for disaster when growing your business is to surround yourself with only those who agree with you.

If no one ever questions your decisions or is concerned about a path forward you are suggesting, proceed with caution. More than likely your people want to speak up but are either too fearful or have been burned in the past to raise their hand.

Your job is to create a culture where people who take what you have and make it better is celebrated.

PRIORITIZE THE RESOLUTION

Turning the negative effects of conflict into positive growth for your business means taking action on what you agree is the wisest path forward for your business. But simply choosing on a path forward isn't enough, you must implement it and take the necessary action steps needed to bring the resolution full circle.

When the implementation and action needed isn't prioritized, momentum wanes and your business ends up in worse shape than it initially started out as. The culture created is one of lip service where conflict resolution becomes a game of good talk and nothing more.

Conflict resolution takes effort, it takes time, and it takes energy. Successfully growing your business in and through conflict means counting the costs and understanding what the investment is prior to starting.

FOLLOW UP

When prioritizing your conflict resolution action plan, ensure you factor in dates for milestones to be accomplished. Growth requires momentum, and the worse thing for the growth of your business is to lose momentum when in the process of resolving conflict.

It's critical to see conflict resolution in your business as your highest priority. The best products and the best services cannot survive in an environment and culture where people do not understand how to overcome the challenges they face with each other.

NEARLY ALL MEN CAN STAND ADVERSITY,
BUT IF YOU WANT TO TEST A MAN'S
CHARACTER, GIVE HIM POWER.

- Abraham Lincoln

Dr. Stephen Kalaluhi

CHAPTER FOURTEEN:
MOTIVATION VS. INSPIRATION

"The journey is never ending. There's always going to be growth, improvement, adversity…"

- Antonio Brown

T here is a common misconception that motivation is synonymous with inspiration. The truth is, nothing could be further from the truth. Business owners who understand the differences between motivation and inspiration, and who learn when and how to deploy each in the process of growing a business, enjoy more success and longer lasting increase.

Using motivation and inspiration interchangeably and without fully understanding how each affects your people, however, has the potential to create the exact opposite results. From a behavioral standpoint, mastering this critical component of growth will unleash your ability to increase your business to any level you put your mind to.

WHAT IS MOTIVATION?

By definition, motivation is an incentive to move an individual or group to action or to impel them to do something.

From a growth perspective, motivation is the process you implement as a business owner to get your people started, to keep them going once they get started, and to keep them focused on achieving a specific and time-bound goal.

Motivation is what you exert on your people as a business owner. When you persuade your people to meet a goal, you are motivating them to achieve it. Typically, motivation is externally derived from either punishment or reward and takes the form of bonuses, loss of jobs, demotion due to lack of performance, etc.

WHAT IS INSPIRATION?

By definition, inspiration is what you do to stimulate to action, to affect or guide, to increase energies, ideals, or reverence.

From a growth perspective, inspiration is the process you implement to help your people imagine something better, to dream about what could be, and to believe it should be your reality.

Inspiration speaks to the drive your people have to excel, to flourish, and to thrive for no reason other than being better tomorrow than they are today. Typically, internally driven, inspiration creates actions that are owned by the individual. These actions are achieved with or without outside influence or assistance and are usually difficult to dissuade or diminish.

WHEN TO MOTIVATE?

Motivation is appropriate and effective when dealing with short-term bursts of higher levels of energy and effort, and when the focus is on repetitive tasks. Using motivation to incentivize higher productivity and increases in output leads to explosive short-term growth.

However, it is important for you as a business owner to understand the boundaries associated with using motivation to grow your company. When used in the short-term, motivational behaviors are an effective method for getting done what needs to get done.

Over a longer period of time, motivational behaviors can exhaust team members who can't see the light at the end of the proverbial tunnel. Giving 110% is great for short bursts, but it's obvious that your people can't continuously give that level of effort and energy before they just drop from over-exertion.

The use of motivational behaviors over long-term periods has the opposite desired effect: Unproductive team members with poorer long-term productivity. This is the root cause of burnout within most businesses, and it is also one of the main culprits of turnover of your employees.

WHEN TO INSPIRE?

Inspiration is appropriate and effective when the goal is to shift your company's culture, or when trying to improve the overall environment.

As opposed to motivational behaviors that focus on accomplishing a task through rewards or punishments, inspirational behaviors focus on personal growth, professional improvement, and the positive outlook of the individuals in the company.

Inspirational behaviors create high-performance teams that are sustainable over the long-term by building environments and cultures that challenge individuals to stretch, increase, and be better daily.

Of the very few downsides associated with inspirational behaviors, the one that causes most business owners to stumble is the amount of time, effort, energy, and resources it requires to inspire well. To inspire each person within your company requires time, it requires you to know who they are as people, to understand their goals and aspirations, and to invest in their future.

GROW YOUR BUSINESS WITH BOTH

Growing your business requires you to effectively and efficiently employ both motivation and inspiration within your company. Use motivation to achieve your short-term goals and reward your people well when they go above and beyond to achieve a goal. Use inspiration daily. Continuously paint of picture in their minds of what could be and what should be. Help them see what you see and challenge them to recognize why it is important they continuously grow.

WE DON'T DEVELOP COURAGE BY BEING
HAPPY EVERYDAY. WE DEVELOP IT BY
SURVIVING DIFFICULT TIMES AND
CHALLENGING ADVERSITY.

- Barbara De Angelis

Dr. Stephen Kalaluhi

CHAPTER FIFTEEN:
STRONG RELATIONSHIPS, STRONG BUSINESS

"No difficulty can discourage, no obstacle dismay, no trouble disheartens the man who has acquired the art of being alive."

- Ella Wheeler Wilcox

Strengthening the relationships with those in your company is a critical behavior you must master if you desire to grow your business. Unfortunately, this is one area where many business owners talk a great game, but very few actually follow through with the steps required to build relationships. The common misconception is building relationships is hard and cannot be accelerated. Here are eight simple keys you can focus on to build strong relationships within your business:

KEY #1: ONE-ON-ONE TIME

You can't strengthen your relationships with your spouse or children if you're always in the middle of a crowded room. The same principle applies to those in your company. You must intentionally and purposefully schedule one-on-one time with each member of your company for the sole purpose of getting to know them better.

KEY #2: CLEARLY COMMUNICATE

Strengthening relationships within your company is next to impossible when what you want and what you need is poorly or ineffectively communicated. As a business owner, you bring light to those things that are important, and when those things are clearly communicated, everyone in your company is aligned with the goal moving forward. Aligned team members are strong team members.

KEY #3: KNOW WHAT IS IMPORTANT TO THEM

If you care about what's important to the people in your business, the people in your business will care about what's important to you. Strong relationships are built upon a common belief that everyone is pulling and rooting for everyone else. One-sided relationships where you expect your people to care about what matters to you, but where you don't care about them is a sure-fire recipe to limiting the growth of your business.

KEY #4: ACTIVELY LISTEN WHEN THEY SPEAK

One of the hardest skills to master as a business owner is the ability to actively listen. Active listening is so much deeper than merely hearing what is said. It is about connecting with the person who is speaking, asking clarifying questions when you aren't sure what you heard is what they actually meant, and summarizing what was shared when the other person is done speaking. To do this well takes time, effort, energy, and focus, but the payoff makes growing your business exponentially easier.

KEY #5: BE THE CALM, NOT THE STORM

Strengthening your relationships is predicated on your ability to keep your team calm, instead of feeding into the chaos. When the craziness of life and work meet head on, you want to be water to the flames instead of gasoline. You keeping a calm head on your shoulders shows your people they can rely on you to be the voice of reason, allowing them to trust you even more.

KEY #6: STEP UP WHEN YOU ARE WRONG

The harsh truth of the matter is no one is perfect, and that includes you. Knowing this truth makes it easier to get things done because you are no longer holding yourself, or anyone on your team, to standards you and they can't possibly meet. When you are wrong, and every time you are wrong, own up to the error quickly and publicly, and do whatever it takes to mend and repair any damage caused by your error.

KEY #7: PRIORITIZE THE RELATIONSHIP, NOT THE WORK

With deadlines and goals and everything that goes into making your business run, it is easy to get caught up in the work at the expense of the relationship. Each goal is tied to a person; each deadline is connected to a person; your day-to-day activities are tied to people. Remembering that these things are tied to people helps you strengthen your relationships because, after all, relationships are tied to people, too.

KEY #8: WALK A MILE IN THEIR SHOES FIRST

The saying goes that you should never judge a person until and unless you've walked a mile in their shoes first. Strengthening relationships is about getting to know your people and getting to know your people is about understanding what they're going through and what they're dealing with. As good as people want to believe they are, performance is negatively affected by their personal struggles. Growing your business means building your relationships, and building your relationships is about you knowing your people and providing solutions to whatever might prevent them from achieving their goals.

THE FRIEND IN MY ADVERSITY I SHALL
ALWAYS CHERISH MOST.

- Ulysses S. Grant

Dr. Stephen Kalaluhi

CHAPTER SIXTEEN:
BUSINESS GROWTH ACCOUNTABILITY

"If you live long enough you will make mistakes. But if you learn from them, you'll be a better person."

- Bill Clinton

ccountability is in such disarray in today's businesses because there's no grey zone when it comes down to it – you are either accountable, or you are not. As a business owner, it is important to recognize this truth in your daily actions and your daily communications, as well as how it affects your ability to grow your business.

You are either accountable to your people or you are not. You are either accountable to keeping your word or you are not. You are either accountable to continuously getting better or you are not. There is no in-between and there is no "almost" when it comes to you being an accountable business owner. These absolutes make it difficult for business owners to stay accountable to the growth of their business and many, therefore, stop trying altogether.

One area that stands to produce the greatest amount of growth in your business is found in accountability. When your people are accountable for their actions, for their behaviors, for their perceptions, and for the quality of their work, your business can't help but thrive. Now, taking this belief system even further, when you are accountable to your people, your business becomes unstoppable. When you are accountable for your actions, your behaviors, your perceptions, and the quality of your leadership, that is when the chains break off and you are released to flourish.

With so much riding on your ability to generate an environment that oozes accountability, why do so few businesses (and their owners) actually practice it?

I personally believe it is because too many business owners have bought into the lie that it is too hard, too challenging, and too difficult to do well. The truth is building a culture of accountability is simpler than most realize. Here are few practical ways to increase and improve the accountability within your business:

BE CLEAR

Summarizing conversations creates clarity within your people. Summarizing conversations builds accountability within your business because it takes the conversation from casual water-cooler talk to executable action items.

Who is responsible for what? By when does it need to be completed? To whom does progress need to be communicated? To whom can they turn to for support? What happens if a timeline is missed?

Asking and answering these types of questions not only creates exponentially more clarity, it creates a level of accountability between two or more people.

BE REAL

Another practical way to improve the levels of accountability within your business is to provide truthful and honest feedback to all your team members, all the time.

Creating clarity is a great way to build accountability within your business. Accountability is solidified, however, when real and honest feedback is given regarding progress and opportunities for growth. When your people take ownership of their growth, or lack thereof, accountability is strengthened within your business.

BE ON-TIME

This tip usually throws business owners for a loop the first time they hear about it. What does being on-time have anything to do with building an environment of accountability?

Well, everything.

When you're late, you are subconsciously telling the other person (or people) that you don't value their time and that they aren't worth yours. When you're late to meetings, late to the office, or late to submit work, what you are telling those around you is the meeting wasn't really that important, the business isn't worth getting to in a timely manner, and the work isn't worth your while. To make matters worse, if you're late to meetings, you're late to the office, and you submit work late, chances are pretty high that your people follow suit.

Being on-time, all the time, shows your commitment to your people and to the growth of your business, points to your integrity as a business owner, and speaks to what you value most. Being on-time all the time is a simple behavior that creates immediate accountability within your business because time is one of the few things that everyone in your business has the same amount to work with.

BE REALISTIC

It's important to remind yourself that building accountability into the culture of your business is a marathon, rather than a sprint. It won't happen overnight, but it will happen if you stay focused on implementing what you're reading right now. Chances are, the culture of your business didn't grow into what it is now overnight, so it's important to have clear expectations related to how much effort, energy, time, and resources it will take to turn this ship.

Building accountability into your culture takes time. Keeping your word once, being on-time once, owning your mistakes once, just won't cut it. A culture of accountability takes time to build, and it takes time to develop.

BE UPFRONT

To build a culture of accountability, you must go first. This starts with being the first to openly own your mistakes. Owning your mistakes not only shows your people that you are willing to admit when you fail, it shows your entire organization that you are holding yourself accountable to meeting and exceeding the expectations and standards they have of you.

It's important that you stop looking at mistakes as failures, and start seeing them as opportunities for growth. Mistakes are simply processes identified that just don't work. Instead of wasting time and energy pointing fingers, assigning blame, or trying to cover them up, learn from them.

BE AN OWNER

This is an interesting subsection to include in a book written specifically for business owners, but unfortunately it is necessary. You see, building a culture of accountability within your business means you own everything that happens, and you take responsibility for your people.

No matter the outcome, you must own it. The project didn't go so well, and your people dropped the ball? Own it. Your team failed to produce expected results? Own it. Miss a key deliverable or due date? Own it. The more ownership you take in regards to what happens within your business, the more control you create around you in regards to getting your folks back on track. This is the truest essence of accountability.

Dr. Stephen Kalaluhi

SHOW ME SOMEONE WHO HAS DONE SOMETHING SPECIAL, AND I WILL SHOW YOU SOMEONE WHO HAS OVERCOME ADVERSITY.

- Lou Holtz

Dr. Stephen Kalaluhi

CHAPTER SEVENTEEN:
GROWTH TAKES COURAGE

"Always seek out the seed of triumph in every adversity."

- Og Mandino

Courageous business owners are few and far between in today's entrepreneurial landscape. The fear of failure, of losing it all, of not making it big looms over business owners and prevents them from achieving the success they know they are capable of.

To grow a business, you must commit to being courageous in your actions, in your words, and in your ownership. Your people need you to be bold enough to stand for what is right, stand for what is truthful, and stand for what is needed. Business owners who exhibit courageous behaviors are quick to make the changes necessary to unlock their company's potential to flourish and thrive.

FACE REALITY

Courageous business owners are willing to face the realities and truths present within their businesses. Courageous owners don't hide behind the lies and falsities because they are easier to hear. Courageous owners get up from behind their desks and listen to what is really going on with their people.

SEEK AFTER (AND LISTEN TO) FEEDBACK

Courageous business owners recognize they have blind spots that prevent them from growing themselves and their businesses. Courageous business owners actively seek out feedback and do whatever they can to reduce or remove those blind spots as they are identified.

HAVE UNCOMFORTABLE CONVERSATIONS

Courageous business owners get good at having the awkward conversations that are intended to correct or align team members who are on the wrong track. Courageous business owners don't sugar-coat the truth. They don't shy away from making the necessary corrections. They don't wait for someone else to handle it for them.

ENCOURAGE PUSH BACK

Courageous business owners recognize that great ideas can come from anyone, from anywhere, and at any time. Courageous business owners encourage their team members to push back on ideas if they have a better, more efficient, or more effective way of completing a task. Courageous business owners are committed to staying open to hearing about and implementing the best idea, no matter who or where it comes from.

ADDRESS UNDERPERFORMANCE

Courageous business owners don't wait for team members to become toxic before addressing performance issues. Courageous business owners are willing to do whatever it takes to protect their companies from anything that might tear it apart. Underperformance, behavioral issues, negative attitudes, conflict within the organization – courageous business owners take immediate action when any of these things arise.

COMMUNICATE OFTEN AND OPENLY

Courageous business owners understand that in order for their teams to make the best decisions they can, they must possess as much information as they can. This means that courageous business owners aren't scared to share information with their people and do so as often as possible to ensure their people are as informed as they can be.

LEAD CHANGE

Courageous business owners never settle for good enough in their growth, in their companies, in their deliverables, or in their people. Courageous business owners constantly look for opportunities to improve and take the necessary steps to implement and execute against those improvements.

STAND BY YOUR DECISIONS

Courageous business owners stand by their decisions and move forward based on their decisions. Courageous business owners understand that they must not only stand on the decisions that they made, but be brave enough to make in-course corrections as often as is required should the circumstances or situations change.

GIVE MORE CREDIT TO OTHERS

Courageous business owners aren't driven by their egos. Courageous business owners are willing to give more credit to others on their team and in their company that they are willing to take themselves. Courageous business owners recognize that giving credit to others is a critical component to growing a business, and they realize that success is less about them and more about their people.

Dr. Stephen Kalaluhi

EXCEED MINIMUM STANDARDS

Courageous business owners don't just meet expectations and standards, they exceed the expectations and standards. They realize that to be an effective owner, they must lead from the front. This means being first to arrive, the last to leave, and constantly setting the bar for the rest of their company to follow.

SCALE

Dr. Stephen Kalaluhi

EVERYONE GOES THROUGH ADVERSITY IN
LIFE, BUT WHAT MATTERS MOST IS HOW YOU
LEARN FROM IT.

- Lou Holtz

Dr. Stephen Kalaluhi

CHAPTER EIGHTEEN:
ALL IN OR NOTHING

"There's always going to be bumps in the road. There's always going to be adversity. You

simply must overcome it."

- Odell Beckham, Jr.

Implementing the constructs found within the pages of this book is no small feat. In fact, most clients I work with commit to a six to nine-month long engagement to do this well. While six months focused on building your business with an additional three months focused on growing your business might seem like a lot of time on the surface, the reality is this part isn't something you want to rush. In fact, taking your time to do the first two parts well is tantamount to positioning you in such a way where you're more likely to succeed when scaling.

On a side note, the building and growing components of this book are mandatory for your success in business. If you fail to implement the aspects associated with the five frameworks of business success, you will struggle. If you fail to improve and enhance the skill sets, mindsets, and behaviors associated with growing your business, your business will plateau.

I bring this up now because, while building and growing your business is an absolute must, scaling your business is not. Scaling your business should actually only be attempted after you have mastered the concepts and constructs outlined in the previous sections of this book.

Why?

Because it's hard to do well and it has the potential to completely ruin what you've built to this point. It has the potential to destroy any growth you've experienced, and it has the potential to eradicate any gains you've made to this point.

100% MINDSET

As you may have guessed, scaling a business is not for the faint of heart. It literally takes all your effort and all your energy to do well. The odds of success are greatly improved when you implement the frameworks of success and the components of growth, but even then, you're not guaranteed to see the fruits of your labor before the tree withers and dies.

With that being said, however, if your goal is to scale your business whether through franchising or opening multiple locations in multiple cities, the underlying force driving this expansion must be one of total and complete buy-in.

That means being totally and completely committed to mastering the five frameworks in this book. That means being totally and completely committed to mastering the ten components of growth. That means exhibiting the behaviors outlined in this text and eating, sleeping, breathing, and bleeding the skill sets, mindsets, and behaviors of building and growing your business.

Anything less will only result in failure. Anything less will only destroy everything you've built. Anything less than your absolute all-in will result in a wasted opportunity, a broken business, and a financially stagnant company.

This is an ominous way to start a section on scaling your business, but it is tantamount to your success that you heed these warnings. Let's take a look at why mastering the five frameworks associated with building a great business and the ten components associated with growing your business are critical to your ability to scale with success.

EVERYTHING SCALES

From a business perspective, the term "scale" is used to describe what happens when a company expands in a proportional way. The key word I want you to focus on in this definition is "expand."

When we think of expanding our business, what most business owners automatically lean toward are images of opening new store fronts, or launching new offices, and taking services nationwide or globally.

While this isn't a bad practice by any means, what most business owners fail to do is think on what happens when you expand faults and shortcomings. You absolutely want to expand your successes, and achievements, and everything that's made you and your company profitable. But the way scaling works doesn't give you the option to choose what expands and what does not.

This is an important concept to understand because expansion affects everything. What you're already good at will expand, but what you struggle with now will also expand. This point is often times overlooked because scaling a business is the new buzz word. It's the shiny new object everyone is focused on. So, they get onboard without really ever counting the costs.

But not you.

You understand that in order to scale successfully, you not only need to focus on making your strengths stronger, you need to shore up your weaknesses and address your opportunities for improvement.

Because here's the truth: If you struggle with a particular area in your business and you're physically there, how much more pronounced will it be translated to an office across the country where you're not?

If you don't have a solid strategy in place, or if your structure is weak, or if you don't have a proper way to proactively stay ahead of industry changes, or if you aren't intentionally developing your people, or if you have a hard time with marketing, how in the world can you expect the situation to improve just because you scale?

You see, it's not just your business model that scales. Your culture, your accountability, your willingness to courageously lead…all these things are magnified when you start the process to scaling. This is why it is critical to approach this from the perspective and mindset of being 100% all-in.

Anything less is setting you up to fail.

OVERCOMING ADVERSITY NOT ONLY MAKES YOU STRONGER, IT MAKES YOU MORE HOPEFUL.

- Valerie Jarrett

Dr. Stephen Kalaluhi

CHAPTER NINETEEN:
THE DUPLICATION PROCESS

"Everyone is handed adversity in life. No one's journey is easy. It's how they handle it that

makes people unique."

- Kevin Conroy

A s mentioned in the previous chapter, scaling a business can be a daunting endeavor. It becomes exponentially more difficult (and more dangerous) when you haven't taken the time to properly take an honest inventory of where you're at as a business owner, what makes up the DNA of your company culture, and what stop-gaps you have in place to ensure what you expect translates throughout every part of the scaling process.

IT IS TIME TO S.W.O.T.

As an assessment, I love the SWOT (Strengths, Weaknesses, Opportunities, and Threats) analysis more than any other. What are the strengths of your business? What are the weaknesses of your business? How can you use those strengths to seize future opportunities? How do your weaknesses contribute to the threats you face? Just answering these four questions is enough to generate a simple plan to scale. That's why I love the SWOT analysis.

The more detailed you can be with your SWOT analysis, the better off your plan for scaling will be. The more specific you can be with your SWOT analysis, the better prepared you and your team will be for what the future holds. Here are a few factors you need to consider when looking at your company's strengths and weaknesses:

Service	Quality	Cost	Speed
Innovation	Technology	Partnerships	Scalability
Sales	Distribution	Retention	Products
Services	Systems	Controls	Operations

While your business may or may not be affected by all the factors listed above, it's important to identify those factors that do affect your business in order to understand 1) whether you consider those factors strengths or weaknesses, and 2) whether those factors affect the execution and attainment of your plan to scale.

The focus of your company's strengths and weaknesses focus on internal processes and factors, but the identified opportunities and threats focus on those factors external to your business. As you go through this exercise, it's is crucial to determine key opportunities and key threats as they relate to the overall success of your team. When you compile your list of key opportunities, the next step becomes understanding how your strengths can be used to seize those opportunities. Opportunities missed represents a failure on your part as a business owner, but not knowing the opportunity ever existed is unpardonable for both you and your team. Keep your key opportunities in the forefront of everyone's minds so that it can be acted upon and grasped when it becomes available. As you look at how you can use your strengths to seize key opportunities, you also want to be cognizant of what steps you can and should take to shore up your weaknesses so they don't prevent you from being able to seize any opportunities that may arise.

In addition to identifying your key opportunities, it is equally important to identify your key threats. Your company's weaknesses exacerbate the identified key threats, so it should go without saying that your responsibility should include creating a plan to shore up your team's weaknesses in order to minimize those key threats. But what makes the key threats less threatening is understanding how your team's strengths can be used to defend against those identified key threats.

TAKE INVENTORY

Completing your SWOT analysis gives you a clearer picture of where you're at as a business owner. More importantly, it allows you to quickly identify those areas that you don't want duplicated as you scale. This process holds the proverbial mirror to your face and forces you to take stock of what you do well, as well as point out those areas where you are possibly at risk.

Here's a ninja-level step that will almost guarantee you scale well:

Perform the SWOT Analysis exercise not only on your business as a whole, but on all five of the building frameworks and all ten of the growth components.

Think about the level of intentionality it would take for you to look at the Strengths, Weaknesses, Opportunities, and Threats associated with your company strategy. Think about how powerful it would be as you scale to conduct a SWOT on the structure of your business. Imagine for a second that you actually performed a SWOT Analysis on how well you communicate, the levels of accountability, your company's culture, or the strength of your teams.

It's a lot a work, for sure. But wouldn't it be worth it to ensure you scaled in such a way that made you more effective, more efficient, and more profitable as a business, rather than the alternative?

YOU LEARN FROM ADVERSITY MORE THAN
ANYTHING BECAUSE IT ALLOWS YOU TO SEE
SO MUCH MORE.

- Draymond Green

Dr. Stephen Kalaluhi

CHAPTER TWENTY:
BECOME A LEAD GENERATION MACHINE

"Prosperity makes friends, adversity tires them."

- Publilius Syrus

N ow that you're in agreement regarding the importance of being all in and having a 100% mindset when it comes to scaling, let's shift our focus and attention to the more practical application and implementation of what it looks like to scale your business, starting with your lead generation and lead qualification process.

YOUR LIFEBLOOD

It should go without saying that leads represent the lifeblood of your business. If you desire to scale your business, your first point of business must be shoring up your ability to generate leads, as well as your ability to qualify those leads you do generate.

While there are several avenues one could go down in regards to generating and qualifying leads, the rabbit hole we're going to jump into is built upon a "customer / client facing" foundation.

START BY BEING CUSTOMER FACING

Let's start this process by addressing the elephant in the room: Your customer / client doesn't care about you. Seriously. They don't give a rip where you went to school. They don't care about your pedigree. They don't care about your certifications, who you've shaken hands with, or anything else you think is important. To be absolutely clear, the only thing a potential customer or client cares about is can you solve their problem.

Scaling your business requires you to create a consistent flow of leads you can then qualify, but most business owners miss the fact that the consistent flow starts from being customer facing.

I encourage you to take a look at your social media presence. Then check out your website. Then flip through your marketing collateral. Chances are pretty high that every one of these business scaling aspects is more about you than it is about your customer. Chances are pretty high that you are vomiting from the mouth your accolades and resume rather than speaking into the challenges they are facing. Chances are pretty high that your customers and clients are bored to death by your website, social media campaigns, and marketing collateral because they can't and don't see themselves in it.

The danger here is pretty straight-forward…if your potential clients and customers don't see themselves in your presentation, they won't connect. If they fail to connect, the act of turning them into paying customers becomes exponentially harder.

Solving the issue of making an immediate connection is as simple as pointing out the greatest challenge your target market is facing. Just talking about your niche's greatest challenge allows you to speak directly into their lives and gives you the ability to meet them exactly where they are at.

Speaking to their greatest challenge sets you up to position your business in the most powerful place you can find yourself in when it comes to selling: A place of empathy.

Demonstrating empathy shows you know how hard it is, and you want to help. You understand what this challenge is doing to their livelihood, and you want to solve it for them. You get what they are going through, and you're willing to do whatever it takes to get them from where they are at to where they want to be.

A customer-facing profile, website, and marketing collateral has the ability to create empathy-based connection and becomes the source of your lead generation. Want to increase the number of leads you generate? Get your message in front of more of those you serve within your niche. Want to generate more leads? Speak precisely to the greatest challenge your target market is facing.

NO MORE TIRE KICKERS

Scaling your business means creating a process that distinguishes between tire-kicking leads and those who are ready to take the next step. In most cases, this process is as simple as offering a lead magnet, or some other kind of complimentary service, product, or value.

Offering something to your leads qualifies them further into your sales funnel because only those serious about addressing the issues preventing them from experiencing life to the fullest will care enough to take the time to download, log on, or a schedule a call. This process automatically identifies for you whom to focus your efforts and energy on, and whom to keep on an email drip nurturing campaign.

Let's say you generate 100 leads tomorrow, and only 10 of those leads take advantage of your free lead magnet or value offering. It's easy to get disappointed that 90 leads didn't have the fortitude to take their growth seriously. But what I prefer to do is rejoice in the 10 who did. Rather than spread your efforts out across 100 leads who have no desire to move forward, you can now focus all your effort on the 10 who do.

Think about how much more effective your closing rate becomes when you're only reaching out to leads who are qualified and into the middle of your sales funnel.

To scale your business, start with creating a customer-facing profile. One that empathizes with your clients' greatest challenge. Then get your message in front of them as often as you possibly can. Offer massive amounts of value to those who choose to connect with you because of the solutions you provide. Give them an opportunity to download something, attend a live virtual training, schedule a call with you, etc. Then go above and beyond to those who are bold and brave enough to take that extra step.

That's what your lead generation to lead qualification process should look like if you desire to scale your business.

ADVERSITY IS THE STATE IN WHICH MAN
MOST EASILY BECOMES ACQUAINTED WITH
HIMSELF.

- John Wooden

CHAPTER TWENTY-ONE:
YOUR MESSAGE, AUTOMATED

"Great things are often birthed from adversity."

- Robert Schuller

As good as you are at connecting with your target market and selling your product or service, your body will eventually require sleep. I tongue-in-cheek tell people that sleep is overrated, but we all know the reality in which we live and the importance of sleep to our ability to function well. What happens to our ability to connect when we're sleeping, though? How does sleep affect our ability to show empathy, to share our hearts, to speak to what we're most passionate about?

If you don't have a proper system in place, the simple answer to the questions asked prior is you miss out. But with a proper messaging program that is available when and where your potential clients are, sleep becomes a non-factor in your ability to connect, empathize, and ultimately sell.

VIDEO IS KING

Video consumption is on a meteoric rise. What this means to you and scaling your business is either you get onto and ride the video wave, or watch as everyone else passes you by. But it's not enough to just post video, you have to stand out. No, I'm not referring to stupid or obnoxious videos that grab people's attention but add no real value. What I'm talking about is using video to give your target market massive amounts of value.

When I share this information in the context of scaling, I typically get one or two questions pertaining to giving away too much value. To which I respond: "There's no such thing…when you do it right."

VIDEO THE RIGHT WAY

When you use video to add massive amounts of value to your target market, you don't have to worry about ever giving too much away when you focus on this ratio:

95% of the video's content speaks to the What and the Why;
5% of the video's content speaks to the How.

Let's break this down so you can see why this is so genius when it comes to scaling your business...

Information is more readily and easily available today than in the entire history of the world. Google has become a verb used to describe what you do when you don't know the answer to something. You can self-diagnose just about any ailment you might have, and you can buy anything your heart desires online.

The videos you create speak to the What of your target market's greatest challenge. For example, my customer-facing LinkedIn profile speaks directly to the challenges coaches, consultants, and B2B solution providers deal with on a daily basis. The video series I created for my target market speaks directly to these challenges. Meaning, I call out the elephant in the room.

What's the greatest challenge facing a coach, consultant, or B2B solution provider? Generating a consistent and reproducible flow of revenue.

My videos address this challenge and call it out. But I don't just stop there. I also speak to the Why of their challenge. What this means is I create a space where I empathize and speak to why it's important this challenge is addressed.

Literally 95% of my videos address the elephant in the room and point out the pain associated with leaving the elephant unaddressed. This approach does a couple of things. First, it positions me as an expert in my niche and builds into my credibility as a solution provider. Not only did I create a video for my target market to watch, I understood enough about their challenges to speak directly to them. Second, these videos allow me to empathize on a level I'm not able to achieve via text. Third, it allows me to provide my target market with massive amounts of value.

Speaking of value, that's where the remaining 5% comes in. Remember, 95% of your business scaling videos focus on What the greatest challenge is and Why that challenge is detrimental to your target market's future, which leaves you with 5% of your video content to speak to the How.

You want to give your niche enough of a taste to make them realize you know what you're talking about and have a solution that addresses their greatest challenge. But for the most part, the How is what your target market pays for.

Information is at the tip of your client's and customer's fingertips. But how to do it is where many lack the skill or accountability to do it well.

Case in point: I can watch YouTube Videos on how to fix a transmission all day long, but without the proper tools or hands-on experience, that information is useless. I would end up taking my car to a mechanic where I would essentially be paying for that mechanic to complete the how portion of fixing my car.

WHEN AND WHERE THEY ARE

Once you have your videos up and ready, literally post them, share them, and attach them to any platform where your target market will see them. Because they are videos, your niche has the flexibility to watch them, absorb them, and learn from them anywhere and everywhere they might be.

Video allows your voice to come through. Your passion becomes more evident in a video, and you create an immediate connection with your audience. These things can be done via written text, but video accelerates this process and gives you the ability to connect no matter the time of day.

Added bonus: When implemented correctly, your videos can easily become a process step in your lead qualification program.

ONE THING I DON'T THINK MY CRITICS
REALIZE IS I'VE BEEN TRAINED TO LOOK
ADVERSITY IN THE FACE.

- Reggie White

Dr. Stephen Kalaluhi

CHAPTER TWENTY-TWO:
STAYING FRONT OF MIND

"I have personally dealt with any adversity in my life with humor."

- Marlee Matlin

The act of scaling your business is the culmination of doing a lot of little things really well consistently over a long period of time. Most business owners forget that scaling a business is a long game, and that everything about scaling needs to focus on long-term gain rather than short term wins.

This mindset shift is difficult for some because the principles outlined in this book have the ability to generate immediate increases in revenue generation. With an influx of cash that wasn't there before, it's easy to get caught up in the now at the expense of what could be and should be 3 years, 5 years, or even 10 years down the road.

Staying front of mind within your target market is one such example of doing the little things well consistently over a long period of time. Blog posts, video shares, follow-ups with qualified leads that didn't buy...these represent business scaling activities, but also are typically the first items to get pushed to the wayside when time is not on your side.

Let's get granular for a moment and talk about consistency and scheduling...

SOCIAL MEDIA POSTING

In today's marketplace, it is considered a sin to not take advantage of multiple social media platforms. My favorites are (in order) LinkedIn, Facebook, Instagram, Twitter. This order is unique to me because I know where my target market lives, so I learned where to invest the majority of my time, effort, energy, and resources. Your list might look different, which is perfectly acceptable so long as you can justify why.

I post daily to LinkedIn and Facebook, and less frequently to Instagram and Twitter. Again, my target market isn't spending time on Instagram or Twitter, so I put forth very little effort in posting there. LinkedIn and Facebook, though, are different stories. I post professional videos and statements on LinkedIn daily, and I post more personable but also professional stuff to Facebook daily.

Like I said before, it's too easy not to post daily, and to not post daily means you're missing out on an enormous opportunity to connect with your target market.

BLOG POSTS

Blogging is an easy win in today's marketplace because it gives you an influencer's voice, even if you don't have one right now. Anyone can write and publish a blog, and with social media platforms like LinkedIn and Blogger, your voice can be shared across the planet with very little effort.

My favorite place to post blogs to is my personal LinkedIn page because of the reach this page has. As of this writing, I have close to 10,000 qualified leads in my LinkedIn circle, and every blog I share gets enough engagement to generate at least one sales conversation per blog.

I write and share blogs to my LinkedIn on a weekly basis. This allows me to share new content each and every week, but it also gives the LinkedIn algorithm something to work with. The newer and fresher your content, the higher you rank on a follower's news feed.

VIDEOS

We spoke in-depth on videos in a previous chapter, but posting videos on weekly basis is a great way to generate and qualify leads. Video truly is king, and the more fresh and new video content you share to your social media platforms, the more relevant you become as a solution provider.

The key to these weekly videos is to take a topic and break it into smaller, bite-sized segments that last no longer than five minutes each. This gives you the opportunity to create video series that keep your profiles fresh and updated with new content.

LIVE MASTERCLASSES AND WEBINARS

On a monthly basis, my company offers our LinkedIn circle the opportunity to join us for live Masterclass or Webinar training sessions. These sessions are powerful, impactful, and transformational, and at no time do we sell. These Masterclasses and Webinars typically reach the system limit of 100 participants because we tell them we're not selling anything. By offering our target market massive amounts of value, we're able to build relational equity which ultimately creates the sales we're after.

These monthly sessions are great as lead qualifiers because they won't sign up if they aren't truly interested. Those who do register not only get your training live, they also get a link to the replay emailed to them. In the body of each email, registrants find a link to the training, as well as a link to schedule time with me or one of our team members.

The purpose of the call is to the help the individual actualize the training in their own business, and to be a resource for them should they have any questions.

During the call, they are asked for permission to share around the programs we offer, and it's only at the point of getting a yes that a selling conversation is entered in to.

Regardless of whether anyone gets on the phone with us or not isn't what's important. What's important is the number of people we as a company are staying in front of.

YOU ARE READY

Scaling your business is simple when you create programs designed to generate consistent flows of qualified leads, build marketing messages that are available when and where your target market is, and stay front of mind with your niche.

These keys, combined with the strategies and foundations outlined in the build and grow sections of this book, represent the secrets associated with creating real and lasting success in business.

REPEAT

Dr. Stephen Kalaluhi

ADVERSITY LEADS US TO THINK PROPERLY
IN OUR STATE, AND SO IT IS MOST
BENEFICIAL TO US.

- Samuel Johnson

Dr. Stephen Kalaluhi

CHAPTER TWENTY-THREE:
DO IT AGAIN

"I'm ready for any adversity that's going to hit."

- Baker Mayfield

S o...now what? You've set into place the frameworks necessary to build a great business. You've established the pillars of growth that every business masters on its way to growing from the inside out. And you've created the systems and processes required to scale your operations, sales, and expansion.

So, what's next? Simple. Do it all over again. That's right. Go back to the beginning of the book and start over again.

Maybe not something you want to hear at this moment, but by this point you must have come to the realization that the principles outlined in this book are not "one and done" principles. These principles are your culture, your lifeblood, your DNA. You can't stop breathing and expect to live for very long. The same should hold true for your business.

So, you implement these principles once...great! But only executing on these principles once is like showering at the beginning of the week and believing you're all set until the following week.

That's absurd, and so is not going back through this book to do it all again.

Take one team through the principles of this book at a time.

Then take one department. Then take one business unit. Then take one...well, you get the idea.

The truly great business owners understand this universal truth:

Building, growing, and scaling your business is your business.

Yes, you have to sell your products and services to keep the lights on and the water running. But let's be real…building and growing and scaling your business is your business. Without this mindset shift and pivot in your belief system, these principles will forever be relegated to nice-to-have status, and only really used when the wheels have fallen off.

When you have an everyday focus on building, growing, and scaling your business, everything else falls into place. You become more profitable because the frameworks are in place to build upon. You become more productive because your leaders are operating on the same level. You become more efficient because your message is staying in front of the right people for longer periods of time.

So, get back to building, growing, and scaling your business.

You owe it to yourself, you owe it to the people you employ, and, most importantly, you owe it to the people you serve.

TRUE SUCCESS IS OVERCOMING THE FEAR OF BEING UNSUCCESSFUL.

- Paul Sweeney

FINAL THOUGHTS AND INSPIRATION

"Fresh activity is the only means of overcoming adversity."

- Johann Wolfgang von Goethe

This book covers everything I wish I knew about building, growing, and scaling a great business when I first launched my coaching practice a few years back. The concepts communicated in these pages were learned the hard way, and if I could go back and start over, I would do so many things differently this time around than I did my first try. I honestly believe that I would have created a six-figure coaching practice years sooner had I implemented what I know now to what I did back then.

But that's the thing about this book. You can read it all you want, but it's not worth anything to you until you start to implement the concepts and suggestions outlined throughout this text. This book was purposefully kept short so as to encourage you to read it multiple times.

Building a successful business is hard work. It takes dedication and commitment, and it requires that you never quit and never stop. This will be my first year of experiencing what a six-figure, multi-office practice looks and feels like, and there are days when I kick myself because I could have been here so much sooner than I did.

What prevented me was the belief that no one was there to help me grow; the belief that no one cared about what I was going through. Here's the thing: you are surrounded by more people in your life who want to see you succeed, than you are by those who will laugh in your face because you failed. The trick is finding and connecting with more of the former than the latter.

But more than finding and connecting with a group of people who want to see you succeed, you have to bring yourself to a place where you're okay with being vulnerable. One of the worst things that comes with the territory of being a business owner is the isolation of not having a real support team that can be your encouragement when you don't feel like you're adequate to do what you're being asked to do.

Being vulnerable means finding a group where you can be open and honest with the struggles you're facing as an owner, and rest in the knowledge that you are not alone in what you're facing. The best thing I ever heard from my support group was, "I'm going through the same thing, so let's figure it out together."

Your support group will keep you accountable to putting these concepts and keys of building credibility into practice; they will support you when you hit that wall; they will keep you focused when you lose sight of why you became a business owner to begin with.

Regardless of whether you find a group today, or find a group next month, it is imperative that you find a group. Your success is dependent on your longevity, and your longevity is dependent on how well you implement the keys outlined in this book, as well as how well you tap into the collective power and wisdom contained within a group of entrepreneurs who have not only been there, but who have successfully overcome the same exact thing you're facing right now.

Stand on their shoulders and create the business you see when you close your eyes and allow yourself to dream. Stand on their shoulders and build the business you desire to have. Stand on their shoulders and accelerate your growth.

You have within you everything you need to build your business as big as you want it to become. The only limitations you face are those limitations you place on yourself. Go out there, build your credibility, and revel in the knowledge that you are positioning yourself to help countless people and countless lives.

MEET THE AUTHOR

Dr. Stephen Kalaluhi

LOOK AT ADVERSITY AS A STEPPING STONE FOR YOU AND YOUR COMPANY'S GROWTH.

- Fred G. Hillman

Dr. Stephen Kalaluhi

IN THE GREATEST OF HUMILITY

"The reward for humility and fear of the Lord is riches and honor and life."

- Proverbs 22:4

A s the President and Co-Founder of K2 Development Systems, Inc., I find convergence in, and am energized by, unlocking people's potential to flourish and thrive. As the host of the nationally televised Business Doctor TV Talk Show, I openly and freely share massive amounts of value with any entrepreneur and business owner willing to listen and implement what they hear.

I believe that my success is a direct reflection of the lives and businesses I have impacted throughout the years, and it excites me to think of the new possibilities and doors that are open thanks in large part to our partnership with EANTV and its distribution to some of the biggest media platforms in the world.

It has been an honor to take you through these four components of creating success in business, and it is my hope that you found value in what you read.

AUTHOR BIO

Dr. Stephen Kalaluhi is the President & Co-Founder of K2 Development Systems, Inc. Dr. Kalaluhi is the creator of San Diego's premier leadership development programs, a certified John Maxwell Team leadership speaker, trainer, and coach, an adjunct professor in Ashford University's Forbes School of Business, a regular contributor for I Love Coaching Magazine, and author of *The Secret to Building High Performance Teams, The Crux of Leadership, CEILINGLESS, The Expert's Guide to Positive Conflict,* and *The Expert's Guide to Communicating Powerfully*, and the book you hold in your hand.

Dr. Kalaluhi helps business owners, entrepreneurs, coaches, consultants, and leadership executives worldwide achieve levels of success not previously believed possible, and indirectly transforms organizations the world over through his ability to transform their leaders. His passion is contagious and his drive is infectious. With more than 15 years of experience as an executive leader, and 6 years of experience as a Non-Commissioned Officer in the U.S. Army, Dr. Kalaluhi's heart for business owners, entrepreneurs, and leaders is built upon the desire to see individuals intentionally and purposefully grow and develop, the desire to help individuals increase their capacity to succeed, and the understanding that individuals committed to their own personal and professional growth positively affect their businesses and organizations.